THE PREEMINENCE
OF CHRIST

PART TWO

THE

I AM

SPENCER STEWART

PROJECT ONE 28

LAWRENCE, KANSAS

The Preeminence of Christ:
Part Two, The I AM

Copyright © 2017 by Spencer Stewart

Published by Project one28
         P. O. Box 442135
         Lawrence, KS 66044

www.ProjectOne28.com

Cover Design: Tyler Norris
         www.tylernorris.me

First Printing 2017

Printed in the United States of America

Paperback ISBN: 978-0-9961867-1-1
ePub ISBN: 978-0-9961867-0-4
Mobipocket ISBN: 978-0-9961867-3-5

Scripture quotations, unless otherwise noted, are from *The Holy Bible, English Standard Version*, copyright © 2001 by Crossway Bibles, a division of Good News Publishers, though always amending the mistranslation "the Lᴏʀᴅ" or "Gᴏᴅ" (in Sᴍᴀʟʟ Cᴀᴘs) to Yahweh or Yah.

Italics in Biblical quotations indicate emphasis added by the author.

PUBLISHER'S CATALOGING-IN-PUBLICATION DATA

Names: Stewart, Spencer Blake, author.
Title: The preeminence of Christ : part two , the I AM / Spencer Stewart.
Identifiers: ISBN 978-0-9961867-1-1 | LCCN 2015935842
Series: The Preeminence of Christ
Description: Includes index and bibliographical references. | Lawrence, KS: Project one28, 2017.
Subjects: LCSH Jesus Christ. | Christianity. | Bible. New Testament -- Criticism, interpretation, etc. | Son of God. | Divine man (Christology). | BISAC RELIGION / Christian Theology / Christology
Classification: LCC BT205.S857 2017 | DDC 232.8 -- dc23

Thanks, God, for Mary Mae Stewart, my grandmother and my earliest memory of faith, teaching me to pray for You to bless all of our family members. Thank You for giving her grace through Your Son to walk the ancient path and start a heritage of faith that continues to impact eternity.

PSALM 115:1 (AT)
Not to us, Yahweh, not to us
But to Your Name give glory
Because of Your loyal love
Because of Your faithfulness

CONTENTS

CONTENTS (CONTINUED)

TABLES

ABBREVIATIONS

AT	Author's translation
BDB	*The New Brown-Driver-Briggs-Gesenius Hebrew and English Lexicon*
BDAG	*A Greek-English Lexicon of the New Testament and Other Early Christian Literature,* Third Edition
c.	*circa*, around (approximately)
cf.	*confer*, compare
CNTUOT	*Commentary on the New Testament Use of the Old Testament*
e.g.	*exempli gratia*, for example
ESV	*The Holy Bible, English Standard Version*
Gk.	Greek (language)
HCSB	*Holman Christian Standard Bible*
Hb.	Hebrew (language)
i.e.	*id est*, that is (in other words)
lit.	literal or literally
LITV	*Literal Translation of the Holy Bible,* Jay P. Green
LXX	Septuagint (Greek Old Testament)
n.	footnote (or, heaven forbid: endnote)
NA[27]	*Novum Testamentum Graece*, Nestle-Aland 27th Edition
NA[28]	*Novum Testamentum Graece*, Nestle-Aland 28th Edition
NASB	*The New American Standard Bible*
NBD	*New Bible Dictionary*, Third Edition
NET	*The New English Translation*
NIDNTT	*New International Dictionary of New Testament Theology*
NIV	*Holy Bible, New International Version*
NKJV	*The New King James Version*
NLT	*Holy Bible, New Living Translation*
p. (pp.)	page (pages)
Pace	Latin: "in peace," employed to express polite disagreement
TWOT	*Theological Wordbook of the Old Testament*
v. (vv.)	verse (verses)

THE NAME

In *Part One*, we saw the abundance of evidence from Genesis through Revelation that the ultimate reason God does everything is the glory of His Name. His Name is a verbal marker that carries His reputation. It signifies His nature, His very Person. Jesus commanded our priority in prayer to be that God's Name be revered as holy, great, and glorious in all the earth as it is in heaven (Mt. 6:9). And God has promised to answer those prayers.[1]

Having learned that God is jealous for His Name to be honored above all things, it feels so unfortunate that His Name has been mistranslated (as "LORD" in small caps) nearly seven thousand times in our English Bibles. We often speak of God's names (plural), but in fact, we mean titles. *God* is a title. *Lord* is a title. Truly, God has only one Name: *YHWH*.

The four consonants of the Name *YHWH* are called the Tetragrammaton or Tetragram ("four letters"). Biblical Hebrew

---

1. E.g., Mal. 1:11-14. See *The Preeminence of Christ: Part One, To the Glory of God the Father* (El Dorado, KS: Project one28, 2012), esp. pp. 1-12, 32, 77 (free at ProjectOne28.com/

was not written with vowels – only consonants.[2] Because the vowels within *YHWH* were not written, and the Jews after the exile stopped pronouncing it (explained below), we cannot be perfectly certain of its pronunciation. However, based on the Hebrew language and the witness of early church leaders' Greek writings, the majority of scholars believe it was pronounced *Yahweh* (yăh'-wā).[3]

God's Name appears 6,823 times in the Old Testament.[4] A shortened form, *Yah*, appears fifty times, including the refrain in the Psalms, "Hallelu*jah!*" We should understand what we are singing: literally, "Praise *Yah!*" Also, many human names contain God's Name within them in significant ways, by which we can understand their missions, such as Elijah ("Yahweh is God") and Micah ("Who is like Yahweh?").

Consider how we treat foreign names. If I had met the Hebrew prophet Samuel, I would not have translated it and responded, "Nice to meet you, Heard-of-God." I would try to repeat it the

---

glory); see also Sam McVay, Jr., and Spencer Stewart, *The Model Prayer: Jesus Said, "Be Praying in This Manner"* (El Dorado, KS: Project one28, 2013), 7-8.

2. Vowel markings were not added until the Masoretes in the 6-10th centuries (see p. 24).

3. Rev. George F. Moore summarizes well, "There is no reason to impugn the soundness of this substantially consentient testimony to the pronunciation Yahweh… coming as it does through several independent channels. It is confirmed by grammatical considerations. The name… enters into the composition of many proper names of persons in the Old Testament, either as the initial element… or as the final element…. These various forms are perfectly regular if the divine name was Yahweh, and, taken altogether, they cannot be explained on any other hypothesis. Recent scholars, accordingly, with but few exceptions, are agreed that the ancient pronunciation of the name was Yahweh (the first *h* sounded at the end of the syllable)" ("Jehovah," *The Encyclopaedia Britannica*, Vol. XV, 11th Ed. [Cambridge: University Press, 1911], 312, available at archive.org/stream/encyclopaediabri15chisrich#page/312/). Cf. J. Barton Payne, *TWOT*, 210; Jeffrey Tigay, *Deuteronomy*, JPS Torah Commentary (Philadelphia: Jewish Publication Society, 1996), 431; note also the "must have been" in *The Jewish Encyclopedia*, ed. Isidore Singer (New York: Ktav Publishing House, 1906), 9:161 (available at jewishencyclopedia.com/articles/11305-names-of-god). For the mistaken "Jehovah," see below, p. 24.

4. *BDB* 217b. Some others say 6,828. I must confess: I did not count! It is worth noting that *YHWH* appears almost three times more often than *Elohim*, "God," which refers to the One true God about 2,340 times.

same way he pronounced it. If I met a Hispanic man named Juan, I would not say, "Nice to meet you, John." And I certainly would not say, "Can I just call you mister?" God Almighty has revealed to us His Name – what grace! There is no more important word in the Hebrew Scriptures than this one – and yet it became avoided and replaced! Because He commanded us to bring it to remembrance forever (Ex. 3:15), with full conviction I declare: we should restore God's Name to our hearts and lips!

Yahweh is the Name above every name, the Name we are to call upon, to love, to praise, to rejoice in, and to magnify.[5] Psalm 9:10 says, "And those who know your name put their trust in you."[6] Therefore, in this volume, we will learn the meaning embedded in the Name Yahweh, so that our trust in Him may be strengthened. Then we will see the multitude of ways in which the Scriptures present Jesus as Yahweh in flesh, full of the same glory, worthy of the same worship. No study could be more important, since the greatest question every person on the planet must answer came from Jesus Himself: "Who do you say that I am?" (Mt. 16:15). Eternal destinies hang on the affirmation or denial that Jesus is the God-Man, Yahweh the Son.

God has promised us a blessing for this endeavor: "In every place where I cause my name to be remembered I will come to you and bless you" (Ex. 20:24).[7] So, I invite you to join me with this cry: "Oh, magnify Yahweh with me, and let us exalt his name together!" (Ps. 34:3).

---

5. Above every name: see the connection of Phil. 2:9-11 to Isa. 45:21-25 on pp. 130-131; call upon: e.g., Gen. 4:26, Joel 2:32, Zeph. 3:9, Rom. 10:13; love: Ps. 5:11, 119:132, Heb. 6:10; rejoice: 1 Chron. 16:10, Neh. 1:11; praise: e.g., Ps. 9:2, 148:13; magnify: Ps. 34:3.

6. I noticed this verse through John Piper, "I Am Who I Am," 16 Sept 1984 (desiringGod. org/sermons/i-am-who-i-am).

7. This Scripture originally applied to God's choice of the place for His tabernacle, then His temple. Now in the New Covenant, the people gathered into Christ are God's temple (1 Cor. 3:16-17, 6:19; 2 Cor. 6:16, Eph. 2:21, Heb. 3:6; 1 Pet. 2:5). *We* are the place where God desires His Name to be remembered. On the Hebrew behind "remembered," see pp. 19-20.

CHAPTER ONE

YAHWEH IN EXODUS 3

The best explanation of the Name Yahweh was given to us in Exodus 3. The people of Israel were abused slaves in Egypt. Moses had been miraculously delivered from the infanticide decreed by Pharaoh. He had been raised and schooled in Pharaoh's household. But Moses tried to deliver his fellow Hebrews in his own power[1] and had to flee Egypt as a murderer. From age forty to eighty, Moses lived in exile in the wilderness as a shepherd, married to the daughter of a Midianite priest. Then everything changed.

EXODUS 3:1-6
Now Moses was keeping the flock of his father-in-law, Jethro, the priest of Midian, and he led his flock to the west side of the wilderness and came to Horeb, the mountain of God. [2]And the angel of Yahweh appeared to him in a flame of fire out of the midst of a bush. He looked, and behold, the bush was burning, yet it was not consumed. [3]And Moses said, "I will turn aside to see this great sight, why the bush is not burned." [4]When Yahweh saw that he turned aside to see, God called to him out

---

1. Cf. Ex. 2:11-12 with Acts 7:25.

of the bush, "Moses, Moses!" And he said, "Here I am." ⁵Then He said, "Do not come near; take your sandals off your feet, for the place on which you are standing is holy ground." ⁶And He said, "I am the God of your father, the God of Abraham, the God of Isaac, and the God of Jacob." And Moses hid his face, for he was afraid to look at God.

God then reported to Moses that He had seen His people's affliction, heard their cries, and had come down to deliver them into the land He had promised to Abraham, Isaac, and Jacob (3:7-9). God told Moses that He was sending him to Pharaoh to bring His people out of Egypt (3:10). The man who had trusted his own abilities forty years earlier had been humbled in the wilderness: "Who am I that I should go to Pharaoh and bring the children of Israel out of Egypt?" (3:11). God responded, "But I am with you…" (3:12, AT).

> Exodus 3:13-15 (AT)
> And Moses said to God, "Behold, I will come to the sons of Israel and say to them, 'The God of your fathers has sent me to you,' and they will ask me, 'What is His Name?' What will I say to them?" ¹⁴God said to Moses, "I AM WHO I AM." And He said, "Thus you will say to the sons of Israel: 'I AM has sent me to you.'" ¹⁵God also said to Moses, "Thus you will say to the sons of Israel: 'Yahweh, the God of your fathers, the God of Abraham, the God of Isaac, and the God of Jacob, has sent me to you.' This is My Name forever, and this is My memorial from generation to generation."

Strangely, some interpreters think God refused to answer Moses. They think this was God's way of keeping His Name mysterious, a way of saying, "I'm too great to be contained in a name." Surely this is incorrect. Consider the obvious meanings conveyed in so many human names in the Bible. Consider the meanings understood in the many titles given to God in Scripture. Would we not expect God's Name to reveal even more glorious meaning? Also, the structure of God's immediate response and the continuing narrative in Exodus prove that God desired this deliverance to give a deeper level of understanding of His Name to the people of Israel and even the ends of the earth.[2] What is more, the question Moses anticipated from the Israelites was more than a request for a sound or a word, which would have been requested in Hebrew with *mî*. Instead, Moses said, "*mₐh* is His Name?" J. Alec Motyer has taught, "In every case where *mₐh* is used with a personal association it suggests enquiry into sort or quality or character…"; even when used of something impersonal, "it consistently demands an exposition of character or inner meaning."[3] The question Moses anticipated "was equivalent to asking: What revelation of God do you bring?"[4] John Durham captures the context well:

> What Moses asks, then, has to do with whether God can accomplish what he is promising…. How, suddenly, can he be expected to deal with a host of powerful Egyptian deities against whom, across so many years, he has apparently won no victory for his people? The Israelites in Egypt, oppressed savagely across so many years and crying out with no letup to their God, have every reason to want to know, "What can *He* do?"….[5]

Durham continued that God's response is more than a mere name: "It is an assertion of authority, a confession of an essential reality, and thus an entirely appropriate response to the question Moses poses."[6]

Notice that God explained His Name with a very helpful structure:

---

2. See the structure explained below and the narrative context in Ch. 3 on Exodus 6:1-8. See also *Part One, To the Glory of God the Father* for God's jealousy that His Name be known in all the earth (esp. pp. 24-30 for the Exodus, free at ProjectOne28.com/glory).

3. "The Revelation of the Divine Name" (Tyndale Press, 1959), 19 (now available free at TheologicalStudies.org.uk/article_revelation_motyer.html).

4. *Ibid.*, 21.

5. *Exodus*, Word Biblical Commentary (Nashville: Thomas Nelson, 1987), 38 (emphasis his).

6. *Ibid.*, 38.

1. "I AM who I AM"
2. "I AM has sent me...."
3. "Yahweh... has sent me...."

In the second and third statements, "I AM" and "Yahweh" are parallel in an otherwise identical expression: "I AM/Yahweh sent me." God did this to explain that the meaning of Yahweh is I AM.

The Hebrew "to be" verb is *hayah*. The three occurrences of "I AM" in verse 14 translate the first person imperfect form of *hayah*, which is *ehyeh*. In Hebrew, the imperfect can communicate either a continuous present tense (more literally, "I am being") or a future tense ("I will be"). Some respectable teachers strongly advocate the translation, "I will be," but as we will see, Jesus clearly interprets it in the present tense as, "I AM," so I suggest we go with Him on this.[7] The parallel shift in verses 14-15 from *ehyeh* to *Yahweh* is a shift from the first person imperfect, "I AM," to the third person masculine singular for when we say it of Him: "HE IS!"[8]

Some reject the explanation "I AM" because it is so basic, so obvious to the Israelites. We should probably keep in mind that most humans throughout history have not believed in the existence of One God, so the evangelistic effectiveness of the Name Yahweh (His expressed goal[9]) is worthwhile. It is not beneath Hebrews 11:6 to include such a simple element in its definition of faith: "that He exists." However basic we think "I AM" to be, it is inexhaustibly glorious. And I suspect there is more here than we first think.

---

7. It is also fashionable to reject the meaning of the Name in terms of God's eternal "Being" because that is supposedly foreign to the Hebrew mind, an importing of Greek philosophy. I do not buy it. See Ps. 90:2, 93:2, 102:27, Hab. 1:12, Job 36:26, esp. Jn. 8:58; Brown, *NIDNTT*, 2:69; Brevard Childs, *The Book of Exodus: A Critical, Theological Commentary* (Philadelphia: Westminster, 1974), 87, citing James Barr, *The Semantics of Biblical Language* (New York, 1961), 58ff.

8. J. Barton Payne, *"yhwh," TWOT*, 211. See also the NET footnote at Ex. 3:14; J. A. Motyer, *The Message of Exodus*, The Bible Speaks Today (Downers Grove, IL: InterVarsity Press, 2005), 70.

9. *Part One, To the Glory of God the Father*, 24-30 (ProjectOne28.com/glory).

Self-sufficiency

God has communicated so much to us by the explanation of His Name as "I AM who I AM." We might start with the reality that He exists eternally, uncreated. Moses sang in Psalm 90:2, "Before the mountains were brought forth, or ever you had formed the earth and world, from everlasting to everlasting you are God."

The classic question from kids, when taught that God made them, is "Who made God?" It was such a joy to teach my kids: "No one made God. God never started. God never had a birthday! God was never born. God has always been alive! God has always been God."[10] Yahweh is the uncaused Cause of all things. He owes His existence to no one and nothing outside of Himself. He is not limited by any standard; He is not defined by others. Our pluralistic, relativistic culture needs to hear: the One true God did *not* answer Moses, "I AM *whatever you say* I AM."[11] HE IS who HE IS, the only eternal, uncreated, infinite God. He does not submit to our whims. We must submit to His unchanging, reality-determining Being.[12]

Why did God appear to Moses in a burning-but-not-burning-up bush? He could have appeared in any manner that He desired. He manifested to Abraham in the form of a man, to Job in a whirlwind, to Elijah in a still small voice.[13] Elsewhere, He is called a "consuming fire."[14] Why now choose to appear in fire that does *not* consume the bush? God does not deal in dumb signs. There must be purpose in this. Normal fire eats bushes. Normal fire consumes the hydrocarbons and leaves ashes.[15] But this fire did not need to

---

10. *Theology 101 for Kids!* (free at ProjectOne28.com/kids).

11. Cf. Piper, "I Am Who I Am" (desiringGod.org/sermons/i-am-who-i-am).

12. "I, Yahweh, do not change" (Mal. 3:6); see more on p. 10 and n. 18.

13. Respectively, Gen. 18:1-2 (see below, p. 65); Job 38:1, 40:6; 1 Ki. 19:12.

14. Dt. 5:24, 9:3, Heb. 12:29

15. Thanks to Veritas Christian School science instructor and Dean of Students, Mr. Ron Krestan, for clarifying.

eat. This fire was its own source. This fire was self-sufficient![16] This portrayed the aseity of Yahweh, the "I AM WHO I AM." In Latin, *a se* means "from Himself."[17] In the fire and in His Name, God reveals to us, in effect, *"I exist because I exist. No one created Me. No one defines Me. No one adds to Me. All that I AM, I AM in and of Myself!"* For example, God does not draw strength from anything, because He is almighty. Even though He does not have to eat to get energy, He never grows weary, never faints, and never sleeps, because He has infinite power and life in and of Himself, in His own Being. God's knowledge does not depend upon anything, because God has infinite knowledge and wisdom in Himself.

The aseity of God, the self-sufficiency of God, has so many ramifications. It means that God never *has* to do something, because He never *needs* anything. Paul evangelized the pagans in Athens with God's aseity:

> ACTS 17:24-25
> "The God who made the world and everything in it, being Lord of heaven and earth, does not live in temples made by man, [25]*nor is he served by human hands, as though he needed anything*, since *he himself gives* to all mankind life and breath and *everything*."

God has no needs. He is all-sufficient in Himself. Because of this, God never changes.[18] There is no imperfection to be shored up and no possibility of Him becoming less perfect than He is. He is Yahweh, the "I AM WHO I AM." Also because God never *has* to do anything to supply some lack, He is absolutely free, totally free to be Himself and enjoy Himself as an infinite Trinity. For example, He did not need to create the heavens or the

---

16. I am grateful for this insight from Motyer, "The Revelation of the Divine Name," 23.

17. This subsection borrows from the author's "The Doctrine of God" (ProjectOne28.com/doctrine-of-God). See also John M. Frame, *The Doctrine of God* (Phillipsburg, NJ: P&R Publishing, 2002), 600-616.

18. Mal. 3:6; Ps. 102:27, Num. 23:19, Jas. 1:17. His divine nature did not change through the Incarnation. See p. 122 on the ancient aphorism, "Remaining what He was, He became what He was not."

earth; He did not need a home. He did not need to create us so He could have someone to love, because "God is love" in Himself, from all eternity: the Father loving the Son and Spirit, the Son loving the Father and Spirit, the Spirit loving the Father and Son, each delighting in the infinite glories of the other Members of the Trinity.[19] God has never been lonely; He did not need to create anything.

But He did create – not out of need, but out of the overflow of His own joy in Himself and His glory.[20] And God remains independent of His creation. Pantheism is false; not everything is God. All created things are totally dependent upon God for existence, but God is not dependent upon anything. God's aseity entails His freedom, which is the basis for our next point, His sovereignty.

SOVEREIGNTY

God's expanded explanation of His Name, "I AM WHO I AM," follows a notable Hebrew structure labeled *idem per idem* ("the same for the same").[21] Some examples help us discover the function of this unique construction. Exodus 16:23 includes the command: "bake what you will bake and boil what you will boil." Notice the same structure as 3:14: verb ("bake"/"boil") plus relative pronoun ("what") plus the same verb ("bake"/"boil"). What is the person going to bake in order to fulfill this command? Whatever she wants. The verb remains unqualified in order to leave it up to the person to bake whatever items she wants to bake. Similarly, Second Kings 8:1 literally commands, "… sojourn where you will sojourn." Where? Wherever she decides.

---

19. E.g., Ps. 16:11, Mt. 3:17, 17:5; Isa. 42:6; Jn. 14:31, 17:23-24, Eph. 1:6, Col. 1:13, Prov. 8:30-31 (cf. 1 Cor. 1:30, Col. 2:2-3)

20. In addition to the verses in the note above, see Ps. 115:3, 135:6, Prov. 8:30-31, Ps. 104:31, Rev. 4:11, Eph. 1:5, 9 (NASB).

21. S. R. Driver, *The Book of Exodus* (Cambridge: University Press, 1929), 362-363. John Piper, "Prolegomena To Understanding Romans 9:14-15: An Interpretation of Exodus

Later in Exodus, God revealed His glory to Moses through His Name, which we will examine more below. The significant point for now is that God, in revealing His Name, again employed the *idem per idem* construction: "I will make all My goodness pass before you and will proclaim before you My Name, Yahweh. And I WILL BE GRACIOUS TO WHOM I WILL BE GRACIOUS, and I WILL SHOW MERCY TO WHOM I WILL SHOW MERCY" (Ex. 33:19, AT). After this verse and other examples, John Piper concluded:

> By leaving the action unspecified the force of this idiom is to preserve the freedom of the subject to perform the action in whatever way he pleases.... Therefore when God says, "I will be gracious to whom I will be gracious and I will be merciful to whom I will be merciful," he is stressing that there are no stipulations outside his own counsel or will that determine the disposal of his mercy and grace. As Childs says, "The circular *idem per idem* formula of the name – I will be gracious to whom I will be gracious – is closely akin to the name in Ex. 3:14 – I am who I am – and testifies by its tautology to the freedom of God in making known his self-contained being."[22]

Before Yahweh explained His Name with the simple, "I AM," He expounded it with, "I AM WHO I AM." He did so to communicate that He is self-sufficient, all-sufficient, and therefore, perfectly free. He is never forced to act. He has everything He needs in Himself, and so He performs any and every action by His absolutely free will. "Our God is in the heavens; he does all that he pleases" (Ps. 115:3, cf. 135:6). John Piper comments, "The implication of this text is that God has the right and power to do whatever makes Him happy. That is what it means to say that God is sovereign."[23] Whatever He wants to do, He does. Because He is the all-sufficient Giver and Governor of all things, He is

---

33:19," *The Journal of the Evangelical Theological Society*, 22/3 (1979), 203-216 (free at desiringGod.org).

22. *Ibid.*, citing Childs, *Exodus*, 596.

never thwarted in doing what He wants to do. To take just a few examples:

> ISAIAH 46:9-11 (NASB)
> ...For I am God, and there is no other;
>> I am God, and there is no one like Me,
> [10]Declaring the end from the beginning,
>> And from ancient times things which have not been done,
> Saying, '*My purpose will be established,*
>> *And I will accomplish all My good pleasure*';
> [11]Calling a bird of prey from the east,
>> The man of *My purpose* from a far country.
> *Truly I have spoken; truly I will bring it to pass.*
>> *I have planned it, surely I will do it.*

> DANIEL 4:35 (cf. Isa. 14:27, 43:13)
>> ...he does according to his will among the host of heaven
>> and among the inhabitants of the earth;
> and none can stay his hand
>> or say to him, "What have you done?"

> JOB 42:2
> I know that you can do all things,
>> and that no purpose of yours can be thwarted.

Moses knew the people would need some fresh revelation of God's nature in order to overcome their despair. Who is their God compared to Pharaoh and the Egyptian gods? Yahweh answered that He is the only One who *Is* – in and of Himself. *In effect, "No one created Me. No one defines Me. No one gives to Me. No one makes Me do anything. I AM sovereign and free to be perfectly Me."* At the revelation of this glorious Name, we can only bow in humbled awe. We see that His uncreated Being is infinitely greater than our creatureliness. He defines everything about our reality. We are utterly dependent upon Him. We can do absolutely nothing apart from Him. If He wills, we will live and do this or that (Jas. 4:13-

---

23. *Desiring God: Meditations of a Christian Hedonist* (Sisters, OR: Multnomah, 2003), 32.

16). May we submit to His self-sufficient sovereignty. May we join in the infinite delight of Yahweh, the great I AM!

Some scholars seem unsatisfied with this explanation of Yahweh's Name – that He is eternal, uncreated, unchanging, self-sufficient, and sovereign. They think this would have been all too obvious to be meaningful in the Exodus context. They think there must be more. My first reaction is that we ought not denigrate what we have seen in this section. It is glorious. It is enough to make our hearts sing now and into the ages. But the context of Exodus does suggest that there is more embedded in the Name of Yahweh. We will look into that in Chapter Three. But first, let us learn some history to answer the question, "Why does God's Name not appear in our Bibles?"

CHAPTER TWO

"LORD"

How on earth do we find ourselves in the situation that major English versions of the Bible do not represent the actual Name of God, but instead replace it with a completely different title?

INTERTESTAMENTAL JEWS

During Old Testament times, God's people wrote, spoke, and sang the Name Yahweh.[1] They even greeted each other with the Name (e.g., Ruth 2:4, Ps. 129:8). But in the intertestamental period (after Malachi, before Jesus), the Jewish people stopped saying the Name Yahweh.[2] There is no explicit evidence for when or why they stopped. The popular explanation is that they feared breaking the third commandment, "You shall not take the name of Yahweh your God in vain, for Yahweh will not hold him guiltless who

---

1. Besides all the Scriptural evidence, it is fascinating to note that the military officer who penned the Lachish Letters during the reign of Zedekiah, king of Judah, frequently wrote *YHWH* (accessible at wikipedia.org/wiki/Lachish_letters).

2. Parke-Taylor, *Yahweh*, 9, 80, 85–88; Payne, "*yhwh*," *TWOT*, 211, 212; Bietenhard pinpoints to the period of Alexander (356–323 B.C., *NIDNTT*, 2:512).

takes his name in vain" (Ex. 20:7).[3] Some ancient Jews claimed the avoidance was motivated by Leviticus 24:10-16, in which Yahweh commanded a man to be put to death for blaspheming the Name.[4] Clearly, the third commandment is the foundation for that action in Leviticus.

However, some scholars disagree with those explanations. Jewish commentator Jeffrey Tigay:

> Avoiding the pronunciation of God's name was an expression of reverence. Philo compares it to the feeling that it is improper to address one's parents by name.[5] There is no evidence for the common view that this avoidance of the name was based on the third commandment. Philo and R. Levi think that it is based on Leviticus 24:15-16.... However, this view is rejected in the Talmud.[6]

Tigay then cited Sanhedrin 56a, which reads, "But perhaps it refers to the pronunciation of the ineffable Name..." – but it then judges that the death penalty of Leviticus 24 only applies if one curses the Name.[7]

However, "reverence" does not seem to tell the whole story. Outside the temple, the Name was substituted with "Adonai," the Hebrew for "my Lord." But in the temple, the priests continued to

---

3. Parke-Taylor, *Yahweh*, 80, quoting A. Murtonen, *A Philological and Literary Treatise on the Old Testament Divine Names*, Studia Orientalia Fennica, XVIII.1 (Helsinki, 1952), 36.

4. "The Names of God – In Rabbinical Literature," *The Jewish Encyclopedia*, ed. Isidore Singer (New York: Ktav Publishing House, 1906), 9:161. See on Philo and R. Levi below.

5. Tigay cites 2 Mos., 207, as well as Kid. 31b; Maimonides, Hilkhot Mamrim 6:3; Shulhan 'Arukh, Yoreh De'ah 240:2; and Sanh. 100a, which alleges Gehazi's leprosy to be punishment for pronouncing Elisha's name (2 Ki. 8:5), though it is clearly for his greed and deceit (5:15-27). Of this reticence to say a parent's name, one wonders, *"What if your heavenly Father commanded you to call Him by Name (e.g., Ex. 3:15)?"*

6. *Deuteronomy*, JPS Torah Commentary (Philadelphia: Jewish Publication Society, 1996), 431.

7. Sean M. McDonough writes, "If the intent of the MT or the LXX of this passage was to prohibit any pronunciation at all of the tetragrammaton, it is remarkable that we

pronounce the Name "as written."[8] Max Reisel reported that after "the death of the High Priest Simeon the Just [c. 198 B.C.] the other priests no longer considered themselves worthy to pronounce the Tetragrammaton distinctly and completely in the daily priestly blessing."[9] However, the historical veracity of this record is suspect because of the questionable rhetoric in context.[10] Nevertheless, at some point, only the high priest uttered the Name, only on the Day of Atonement, and cautiously. Of the transition to absolute prohibition, Abraham Cohen wrote:

> Behind the care not to give explicit utterance to the Name may be detected a lowering in the moral standard of the priests. The Talmud declares: "At first the High Priest used to proclaim the Name in a loud voice; but when dissolute men multiplied, he proclaimed it in a low tone" (p. Joma 40d).[11]

The underlying concern seems to be protecting the Name from being profaned by vain speech, à la Exodus 20:7, even from priests.

Eventually, utterance of the Name was completely prohibited in the strongest terms possible: the Talmud records the teaching of Abba Saul, "Whoever pronounces the Name forfeits his portion in the future world" (Sanh. xi. 1, *contra* Mt. 12:31). Contextually, though, it is possible that he made this statement in reference to those who pronounced the Name in a magical curse against their enemies, not in true piety.[12] Sean McDonough reports, "The

have no record of anyone using them for this purpose" (*YHWH at Patmos: Rev. 1:4 in Its Hellenistic and Early Jewish Setting* [Tübingen: Mohr Siebeck, 1999], 112, emphasis his).

8. Sot. VII, 6; Abraham Cohen, *Everyman's Talmud* (New York: E. P. Dutton & Co., 1932), 26.

9. *Observations on 'ehyeh ªsher 'ehyeh (Ex.III.14), hu'h' (D.S.D. VIII.13) and shem hamm^ephorash* (Assen: Van Gorcum & Comp., 1957), 64, qtd. in Parke-Taylor, *Yahweh*, 86.

10. See McDonough, *YHWH at Patmos*, 101-102.

11. *Everyman's Talmud*, 26. Cf. *The Jewish Encyclopedia*, 9:163.

12. See McDonough, *YHWH at Patmos*, 103-104. Either way, it was the opinion of one rabbi, not Jewish law, as often represented in other resources.

widespread use of variations of the divine name in magic shows that this was a very real problem in the Jewish community," and others agree this surely played a part in the prohibition.[13]

The Jews did not stop with YHWH; they also came to consider *Adonai* to be too holy to be uttered, so they substituted for it *hashem*, "the Name."[14] In the Targums, *memra*, "Word," frequently stands in for the Name.[15] William Albright explained this as "a period when influential Jewish groups were engaged in 'building a fence' around the holiness of God, by substituting words denoting aspects or qualities of Him, such as Divine Wisdom, the Divine Word, the Divine Presence... for his Divine Name."[16]

In a thoroughly researched dissertation, Sean McDonough described the frustrating reality: "We must say from the outset that we have no direct evidence to tell us precisely when and why the practice of not using YHWH was introduced."[17] Having surveyed the evidence, he summarized:

> In each of the areas discussed – blasphemy, oaths and curses, and magic – there were compelling theological and sociological reasons to restrict the use of the divine name.... We would submit that the misuse of the name in these areas was the engine which pushed forward the more wide-ranging restrictions on the name. When we read in the rabbinic texts that the name was taken from Israel because of their "unworthiness," this may reflect the abuse of the name in the ways we have discussed.[18]

In the transition, it seems that a substitute version of the Name, represented in Greek as *Iaō*, was shared with Gentiles.[19]

---

13. *Ibid.*, 112. Cf., e.g., Moore, *The Encyclopaedia Britannica*, Vol. XV, 311.

14. Parke-Taylor, *Yahweh*, 87.

15. *Ibid.*, 88. The Targums are interpretative renders of the Hebrew Scriptures into Aramaic (see Bruce M. Metzger, "The Jewish Targums," http://www.bible-researcher.com/aramaic4.html).

16. *From Stone Age to Christianity*, 2nd Ed. (Baltimore: John Hopkins, 1946), 285, qtd. in Parke-Taylor, 88. "Building a fence" was the Jewish description, considered wise piety.

17. McDonough, *YHWH at Patmos*, 111.

"Yet it is certain that some Jews, and probably most Jews, did keep the name hidden from those outside the community. One might say that as the national borders of Israel dissolved, the borders around the name were tightened in compensation."[20]

We must keep in mind that, even once prohibited from general use, the Name continued to be pronounced for some time in the temple, keeping the holiest Name in the holiest place with the holiest Jews (priests). McDonough argues that "we must see this in light of the overall consolidation of power by the temple authorities. It is one piece of the larger puzzle. Having the exclusive rights to say the name would have been of inestimable value for the powers in Jerusalem."[21]

Absent a clear explanation for the prohibition in the historical evidence, McDonough's deductions seem quite reasonable:

> We might venture to say that the restriction of the name was precipitated by its abuse in blasphemy, oaths, etc., and that this restriction was furthered by social factors such as consolidation of power in the temple, and the preserving of national identity in a new cultural and political environment. In any case, we cannot simply say that it was the result of "reverence" or "superstition," although no doubt these two factors were important in perpetuating the restrictions on saying the name in everyday life.[22]

We can definitely agree with the Jews of that period that the Name of God is holy and worthy of the utmost reverence. But were they correct to stop speaking the Name aloud? No. *By avoiding the Name Yahweh, they violated God's command in Exodus 3:15: "This is My Name forever,[23] and in this manner I am to be remembered*

---

18. *Ibid.*, 113.

19. See, *ibid.*, 119-122, where the possible vocalization is given as *Yahô͏ͤh* or *Yahû͏ͤh*.

20. *Ibid.*, 114.

21. *Ibid.*, 113.

22. *Ibid.*, 115-116.

throughout all generations" (AT). The Hebrew for "remembered" connotes more than merely an internal thought; it includes the idea of bringing to remembrance by *speaking aloud*. In worship contexts, it is "equivalent to the name of Yahweh pronounced, proclaimed out loud."[24] *According to Yahweh in Exodus 3:15, we should be pronouncing His Name still today and forever.*

The priests also disobeyed the commands in Numbers 6:22-27 to bless the people of Israel by speaking God's Name over them. The verbal necessity is so clear:

> Yahweh spoke to Moses, saying, [23]"Speak to Aaron and his sons, saying, Thus you shall bless the people of Israel: you shall say to them,
>
> > [24]Yahweh bless you and keep you;
> > [25]Yahweh make his face to shine upon you and be gracious to you;
> > [26]Yahweh lift up his countenance upon you and give you peace.
>
> [27]"So shall they put my name upon the people of Israel, and I will bless them."

Besides priests, ordinary Israelites had blessed others in the Name Yahweh in course of ordinary life (e.g., Ruth 2:4, Ps. 129:8). Every Israelite was called to love and praise the Name of Yahweh. They were given a Spirit-breathed hymnal – Psalms, full of the Name Yahweh – to be sung in corporate worship. They were commanded to "call upon the Name of Yahweh."[25] Paul van Imschoot teaches

---

23. The Talmudists even sought to justify the prohibition by changing the "forever" in Ex. 3:15. It is clear from context that they knew the true reading (*l'ōlām*), but they changed it to *l'allēm* ("to conceal"). Parke-Taylor, *Yahweh*, 86 and n. 45; *The Jewish Encyclopedia* says it was "written defectively," 9:162; cf. McDonough, *YHWH at Patmos*, 108, n. 252. Rather, the Talmudists should have feared Deut. 4:2 and 12:32.

24. Durham, *Exodus*, 40, crediting Schotrroff, cf. Childs. John Currid, "... it carries a more specific meaning of invocation, proclamation and praise" (*Exodus*, Vol. 1 [Auburn, MA: Evangelical Press, 2000], 92).

25. Gen. 4:26, Ps. 116:13, 17; Joel 2:32, Zeph. 3:9, Zech. 13:9, cf. Ps. 99:6, 105:1

that this phrase literally means "to cry by the name of Yahweh," in other words, "to call on Yahweh by pronouncing the divine name with a loud voice in an act of public worship."[26] What is more, Israel was commissioned to invite all peoples to bless Yahweh.[27]

An alarming strand of Scriptures shows that the Israelites were supposed to avoid taking on their lips the names of false gods, not the Name of Yahweh (Ex. 23:13, Josh. 23:7, Ps. 16:4). Failing to bring to remembrance the Name of Yahweh was considered a fruit of apostasy (Jer. 23:27) and God's punishment for idolatry (44:26). The New Covenant promise included God's sovereign grace to remove the names of the Baals from their mouths, so they may again call upon the Name of Yahweh (Hos. 2:17-23, Joel 2:32). Indeed, in the age to come, the Name Yahweh is promised to be the One Name on His people's lips (Zech. 13:2, 14:9), and even Gentiles will learn to take oaths by His Name: "As Yahweh lives..." (Jer. 12:16, 4:2).

For all of these reasons, I believe the Jews who outlawed pronouncing the Name sinned against God and did a great disservice to all the generations who followed them. The Jews in that period were "building a fence." They were adding their own rules around the true commandments of God, trying to ensure proper reverence. They were so "spiritual." At least, they loved to be seen as spiritual (e.g., Mt. 6:5, 23:27-28). The practice of substituting "Adonai" for *Yahweh*, in direct disobedience to Exodus 3:15 and other Scriptures, reminds me of what Jesus said of the Pharisees in a similar context: "And why do you break the commandment of God for the sake of your tradition? ...So for the sake of your tradition you have made void the word of God" (Mt. 15:3, 6).[28] It

26. *Theology of the Old Testament, I: God*, Trans. Kathryn Sullivan and Fidelis Buck (New York: Desclée Company, 1965), 183, qtd. in Parke-Taylor, *Yahweh*, 14, fn. 68.

27. E.g., Ps. 57:9, 96:7, 96:10, 102:22, 105:1, 108:3, 117:1

28. The Jews admitted that "because the people had neglected the Torah, it was necessary to 'make void the Law,' i.e. retract the practice of greeting with the name (cf. t. Ber. 7:23)" (McDonough, *YHWH at Patmos*, 104, in discussion of M. Ber. 9:5 on Ruth 2:4).

reminds me of King Saul and his people disobeying the command to destroy everything, so they could do the "spiritual" activity of sacrificing the best Amalekite sheep to God (1 Sam. 15:15). It reminds me of Ahaz disobeying God's command to ask for a sign in the cloak of piety, refusing to test God (Isa. 7:12). Disobedience in the guise of reverence is not spiritual, but carnal. Avoiding the Name Yahweh was made-man religion. I suggest we do not follow their example.

Two qualifications. First, in the presence of an unbelieving or Messianic Jew who considers it irreverent to say the Name, I would try to avoid it as well, not wanting to offend before making the most of the opportunity to minister the truth in love (1 Cor. 10:32-33). Paul became like a Jew under the law to win Jews under the law, even though he regularly lived free of it (9:19-23, cf. Gal. 2:14). Paul did not eat meat sacrificed to idols in the presence of an idolater or a weak brother, but he did eat it on his own or with the strong: "For why should my liberty be determined by someone else's conscience?" (1 Cor. 10:29, cf. Rom. 14-15). I commend sensitivity, but I do not believe the weak conscience of potential hearers of our public ministries should stop us from obeying the Scriptures to exult in the Name of Yahweh and invite all peoples to join us.

The second qualification makes clear that none of my words above should be misconstrued as or used to justify anti-Semitism. Yes, I believe the Jewish leaders led the people astray in forbidding the Name and thereby impoverished us all. But it is possible for God to rebuke and judge leaders while promising loving correction for His people (e.g., Ezek. 34). We should share His compassion, longing for His people to be freed from the man-made fence in order to praise and promote His Name, known most fully in *Yeshua Messiah,* Jesus Christ. That day is coming (Rom. 11:25-27), and we better be found agreeing with God's plan for Israel without prejudice in our hearts.

THE SEPTUAGINT

The Old Testament was originally written in Hebrew and Aramaic. The standard Greek translation of the Old Testament was called the Septuagint (LXX), according to the tradition that seventy elders translated it in the third century B.C.[29] The New Testament writers and early church fathers clearly quoted from the Septuagint frequently (though sometimes it seems they created their own Greek translations from the Hebrew).

The earliest LXX manuscripts show the Tetragram written in Hebrew script in the flow of the Greek text![30] However, because the Jews of this period were speaking "Adonai" instead of "Yahweh," the majority of Greek manuscripts replaced *YHWH* with *Kurios*, which is Greek for *Adonai* and also means "Lord." This has massive significance for understanding the New Testament and our English translations, as we will see. The clumsiness of this decision by the Greek scribes is evident in places where the Hebrew combined *Yahweh* and *Adonai* in a compound designation of God. For example, in Deuteronomy 3:24, Moses addressed God as *Adonai Yahweh*, but the LXX redundantly rendered it *Kurie Kurie*, "Lord, Lord."[31]

THE MASORETIC TEXT

The Masoretic Text "forms the basis for our modern Hebrew Bibles and is the prototype against which all comparisons are made in Old Testament textual studies."[32] The Hebrew *masora*

---

29. Mark R. Norton, "Texts and Manuscripts of the Old Testament," *The Origin of the Bible*, ed. Philip Comfort (Carol Stream, IL: Tyndale House, 2003), 168-169.

30. Parke-Taylor, *Yahweh*, 84; Bietenhard, *NIDNTT*, 512.

31. In Exodus 23:17, the Hebrew is *Adonai Yahweh*, which the LXX paraphrased as *kuriou tou theou sou*, "the Lord your God." (The Hebrew for God, *el* or *elohim*, is not actually present.) In Genesis 15:2 and 8, Abram twice addressed God has *Adonai Yahweh*, but the LXX rendered it inconsistently as only *despota* in verse two and *despota kurie* in verse eight.

32. Norton, "Texts and Manuscripts of the Old Testament," 158.

means tradition. The Masoretes were Jewish scholars at Tiberias, on the Sea of Galilee, whose "school flourished between A.D. 500 and 1000."[33] Remember that the original Hebrew used only consonants and no vowels. The Masoretes added vowel pointing to the Hebrew Scriptures. Because of the traditional substitution of *Adonai* for *Yahweh*, the Masoretes added the vowels of *Adonai* to the consonants of *YHWH* as a reminder not to pronounce the divine Name. This confused some later translators.

JEHOVAH

If taken literally, the original Hebrew consonants with the substitutionary vowel pointing produced an entirely new word. "The earliest appearance of this transliteration we find in two passages of the 'Pugio fidei.' 1278, though it is not improbable that this is due to a later copyist. We know for certain, however, that this misnomer was brought into prominence by Petrus Galatinus, confessor of Leo X,"[34] who wrote his chief work in 1516. In 1530, William Tyndale first translated the Bible into English and in several verses rendered God's Name as *Iehouah*.[35] (The affricative "J" and "V" did not enter the English language until later, so it was pronounced like we would now spell "Yehowah." The original "J" sound remains in some words, such as hallelu*j*ah.) "Jehovah" appears four times in the King James Version, consistently in the American Standard Version, and often in popular church culture. However, J. Barton Payne, along with others, calls this rendering "impossible."[36] Though mistaken, we should appreciate the attempt to transliterate the Name rather than substitute a different title.

---

33. *Ibid.,* 158.

34. Hans H. Spoer, "The Origin and Interpretation of the Tetragrammaton," *American Journal of Semitic Languages*, XVIII (1901), 30, qtd. in Parke-Taylor, *Yahweh*, 9, fn. 49.

35. E.g., Ex. 6:3 (biblestudytools.com/tyn/exodus/6.html, where it can be seen that he most often translated YHWH as "Lorde").

36. *TWOT*, 211. Colin Brown: "a misunderstanding", "a malformation... never actually used as a word" (*NIDNTT*, 2:69-70). *The Jewish Encyclopedia*: "a philological impossibility" (9:160).

Modern English Bibles

The Jerusalem Bible, a Catholic translation (1966), may have been the first English version to translate the Name as "Yahweh" instead of "Jehovah" or "Lord." However, in 2001 and 2008 the Vatican forbade the use of the Name in services.[37] All major English translations today, Catholic and Protestant, regularly mistranslate *YHWH* as "Lord" in small capital letters. The normal lowercase spelling of "Lord" represents an accurate translation of *Adonai*. I typically take students to Psalm 110:1 to easily see the difference: "The Lord said to my Lord" signifies, "*Yahweh* said to *Adonai*."

However, in the New Testament quotations of Psalm 110:1 (e.g., Mt. 22:44), these versions use lowercase letters for both words, "The Lord said to my Lord," because they are translating the Greek New Testament, which read, "The *Kurios* said to my *Kurios*." Therefore, as we are studying New Testament quotations of the Old, we need to flip back to the Old Testament to see if it contains "Lord" or "Lord" so we can know if the passage originally contained *Yahweh* or *Adonai*. The significance of that exercise will become more apparent in Chapters Six and Seven.

Because *Adonai* and *YHWH* often appear together, rather than mistranslating, "the Lord Lord," most versions adjust the mistranslation to "the Lord God" (e.g., Dt. 3:24), again with small caps representing the Hebrew *YHWH*. In this, the translators are following Jewish practice represented in the Masoretic Text, which placed vowel pointing for *Elohim* ("God") over the Tetragram in these cases instead of the vowels for *Adonai*.[38] Thus they read aloud, "*Adonai Elohim*" (my Lord God). The NASB renders *YHWH* as "God" 314 times. NIV, on the other hand, shifts the translation of *Adonai* in these instances to render the phrase, "the Sovereign Lord."

---

37. "Vatican Says No 'Yahweh' In Songs, Prayers At Catholic Masses," 26 Aug 2008 (catholic.org/news/ae/music/story.php?id=29022).

The main justification for this mistranslation is that the New
Testament writers themselves followed the LXX in substituting
Kurios for *YHWH* in their Old Testament quotations. This is a
noteworthy accommodation to the accepted practice and version
of the Scriptures in their day. Because of this, we have no way of
knowing whether or not Jesus or the apostles ever said the Name
Yahweh. Jesus clearly knew Aramaic (Mt. 27:46), probably also
Hebrew. He surely spoke in His native tongue to His disciples and
probably also in His debates with the teachers of the Law in the
temple and synagogues. But our sovereign LORD saw fit to breathe
His Scriptures in Greek, so we cannot know with certainty.

But because Jesus – preeminently concerned with the glory of
God's Name – fulfilled the Scriptures with perfect obedience,[39] I
cannot believe that He violated God's command in Exodus 3:15 to
be remembered by the Name Yahweh throughout all generations.
I believe Jesus spoke, "Yahweh," but I will have to ask Him when
He returns. As far as I can tell, the earliest record we possess of
a Christian using the Name is Clement of Alexandria (c. 150–
215).[40]

One of the perceived benefits of mistranslating with "LORD"
is that it helps connect the New Testament use of "Lord" for Jesus
with the God of the Old Testament. We will engage in that exercise
in Chapters Six and Seven, and it will be glorious. However, to
me, it does not justify mistranslating *the Name* with a *different title*
in disobedience to Exodus 3:15. I consider it better to educate
disciples about the Name Yahweh, the Jewish avoidance, the Greek
substitution, and its effect on the New Testament manuscripts.

---

38. Tigay, *Deuteronomy*, 431; *The Jewish Encyclopedia*, 9:160.

39. Mt. 3:15, 5:17-20, cf. also Jn. 17:6

40. Payne, "*yhwh*," *TWOT*, 211. Theodoret, who died c. 457, reported that the Samaritans
    pronounced it *Iabe*. Rev. George F. Moore, writing in 1911, "Finally there is
    evidence from more than one source that the modern Samaritan priests pronounce
    the name Yahweh or Yahwa" ("Jehovah," *The Encyclopaedia Britannica*, Vol. XV,
    11th Ed. [Cambridge: University Press, 1911], 312, available at archive.org/stream/
    encyclopaediabri15chisrich#page/312/).

I rejoice that use of the Name Yahweh has increased recently in teachings, songs, and even Bible translation. The *Holman Christian Standard Bible* (2010) transliterates the Name, occasionally. One of its editors explained:

> …the HCSB wanted to introduce to modern English readers the rendering of the divine name used by most Old Testament scholars, which is Yahweh. We felt it was time to depart from treating "the LORD" as if it were a name in such verses as Exodus 33:19: "I will proclaim before you my name 'The LORD'" (RSV). In the first edition, however, rather than a wholesale changing of LORD to Yahweh, we were very tentative or conservative in the number of times we used Yahweh, settling for about 75. The positive response we received to that decision encouraged us to use God's name much more in the updated edition (about 600).[41]

I celebrated the step in the right direction. Unfortunately, in the updated version (2017), the committee removed all instances of "Yahweh." They wanted to be consistent with "LORD" (consistently wrong) and relayed that "feedback from readers also showed that the unfamiliarity of 'Yahweh' was an obstacle to reading the HCSB."[42] Obviously, I find it sad that major translators have to consider sales in the way that they do and choose to mistranslate rather than educate the Church.

I hope we soon see good, literal translations that exclusively render *YHWH* as *Yahweh*. Until then, I have trained my mind into the habit of thinking and saying "Yahweh" when seeing "LORD" or "GOD," and I encourage others to do the same.

---

41. E. Ray Clendenen, "When and Why Do We Update Bible Translations?" (biblegateway. com/perspectives-in-translation/2010/12/when-and-why-do-we-update-bible-translations-e-ray-clendenen/). They feared consistency "would make the Bible seem too uncomfortable for most people" (in A. Roy King, "New Translation of Holman Bible Increases Use of Yahweh," 23 Nov 2010 [aroyking.wordpress.com/2010/11/23/new-translation-of-holman-bible-increases-use-of-yahweh-in-its-text/]).

42. Tom Schreiner in Daniel Motley, "Why Update a Beloved Translation? An Interview with Tom Schreiner," 23 Jan 2017 (blog.logos.com/2017/01/interview-tom-schreiner-christian-standard-bible/).

CHAPTER THREE

YAHWEH IN EXODUS 6

We saw in Chapter One that God chose one Name, Yahweh, to communicate that He is eternal, uncreated, unchanging, self-sufficient, and sovereign. Though we are blown away by this revelation, we noted that some consider that too simple and press for more meaning in the Exodus context.

Many of them stress the Presence of God, promised in 3:12, when God responded to Moses' insecurity with, "But I am with you" (AT).[1] This, too, is glorious. Central to the Scriptural storyline is the desire of the holy God to be present with image-bearers on earth, even sinful ones, from Adam to Enoch, Noah, Abraham, Isaac, Jacob, and Joseph.[2] However, Exodus 6:1-8 teaches that God intended a revelation of His Name that surpasses what the patriarchs experienced, so we must look for more than the gracious Presence that they, too, enjoyed.

---

1. The Hebrew imperfect could be future or present continuous. Future tense would be natural here, but present is chosen to show its parallel to Ex. 3:14 (see p. 8 for it).

2. Gen. 3:8, 5:22, 6:8-9, 21:22, 26:24, 28; 28:15, 31:3 39:2-3, 21, 23 (Acts 7:9), Rev. 21:3.

REDEMPTION THROUGH JUDGMENT

At the end of Chapter One, a paraphrase was offered of the revelation Moses brought to his people. More from Exodus 3 can be added to it. They could trust their God because He said, in effect, "No one created Me. No one defines Me. No one gives to Me. No one makes Me do anything. I AM sovereign and free to be perfectly Me. *And what I want to do is deliver you from your slavery by judging your enemies and then fulfill My covenant with your fathers to grace you with the promised land.*"[3] Therefore, when the people heard the report from Moses and Aaron, "The people believed; and… they bowed their heads and worshiped."[4]

Yet when Moses and Aaron first confronted Pharaoh, the king retorted, "Who is Yahweh that I should obey his voice and let Israel go?" (5:2, a very foolish thing to say). Pharaoh not only refused to release the Israelites, he also increased their workload impossibly and had their foremen beaten for not achieving the new quota (5:6-18). The leaders blamed Moses for this "evil" and called on Yahweh to judge him for it (5:19-21).

> Then Moses turned to Yahweh and said, "O Lord, *why have you done evil* to this people? Why did you ever send me? [23]For since I came to Pharaoh to speak in your name, *he has done evil* to this people, and you have not delivered your people at all" (5:22-23).

In this fascinating prayer, Moses (who was blamed for the evil) rightly attributed the action to Pharaoh, "*he* has done evil to this people" (v. 23), yet under the providential hand of Yahweh, "why have *you* done evil to this people?" (v. 22). The psalmist would later memorialize the Exodus with the same compatibility between human responsibility and Yahweh's sovereignty: "He [Yahweh] turned their hearts [the Egyptians'] to hate his people, to deal

---

3. See Ex. 3:7-10, 16-22.

4. Ex. 4:31, in response to the report of 4:30.

craftily with his servants" (Ps. 105:25). Whatever evil Pharaoh and his servants did, Yahweh could have prevented it, and Moses asked for an explanation.

> But Yahweh said to Moses, "Now you will see what I will do to Pharaoh, for with a strong hand he will let them go, and with a strong hand he will drive them out of his land" (Ex. 6:1, AT).

Well, Yahweh had said that earlier, and it did not turn out so well. How could Moses and the Israelites trust this? Because God followed this promise with His own motivation to uniquely make known His Name, Yahweh, by redeeming His people through judgment upon their enemy.

> EXODUS 6:2-3
> God spoke to Moses and said to him, "*I am Yahweh.* ³I appeared to Abraham, to Isaac, and to Jacob, as God Almighty, but by *my name Yahweh* I did not make myself known to them.

If the sovereign Yahweh is determined to magnify His Name through a specific event, we can be certain it will take place according to plan.

THE PATRIARCHS

Liberal scholars seized upon the sense in the unhelpful translation, "*by* My Name Yahweh I did not make Myself known to them" (6:3). They take this to mean that no one had heard of the Name Yahweh before Moses. Yet the Name is scattered throughout Genesis, as early as when Adam was living as grandfather to Enosh (Gen. 4:26). Therefore, liberal textual critics concocted the Documentary Hypothesis. Applying evolutionary theory to the development of religions and literary works, they alleged that the first five books of the Bible were not written by Moses, but by four redactors who added their own emphases. Supposedly, the "Yahwistic editor" added the Name Yahweh into older stories, even though those characters did not yet know the Name.[5]

First of all, this rank speculation is in opposition to Jesus, who said that Moses wrote these books.[6] The liberals counter that Jesus simply accommodated to the misperception of His contemporaries, even though He knew better. But seriously, what we know of Jesus' character and controversial actions prove that He was not prone to accommodation, but holy confrontation (overturning moneychanging tables) and correction ("you have heard it said, but I tell you"; "Why do you break the command of God for the sake of your tradition?").[7] Many other Scriptures also attribute authorship to Moses, and they are God-breathed and inerrant.[8] Thankfully, the scholarly tide has turned recently against the Documentary Hypothesis.[9]

Contextually, if Moses had returned to Egypt with a never-before-heard Name of God, how would that validate him before the Israelites? They could easily dismiss him as a fake who makes up fake names. We learned earlier that Moses had not used the Hebrew that asks for a mere audible designation; he used the Hebrew that inquires about the inner nature and character represented by the Name. He did not ask God for a two-syllable sound that the Israelites had never heard; he asked for fresh revelation of God's character communicated by the sound with which they were already familiar.

Therefore, the translation "*by* My Name Yahweh" is not helpful, because it leads us to think in terms of mere vocalization. In truth, the English "by" is not representing the original Hebrew. There is no Hebrew preposition before "My Name Yahweh." This

---

5. See Motyer, "The Revelation of the Divine Name," 2-11; Norman L. Geisler, *Baker Encyclopedia of Christian Apologetics* (Grand Rapids, MI: Baker Books, 1999), 586-588; John D. Currid, *Genesis*, Vol. 1 (Darlington, England: Evangelical Press, 2003), 23-33.

6. E.g., Lk. 20:37 (*about Ex. 3!*), Mk. 7:10 (about Ex. 20:12), Jn. 5:46, 7:19-23.

7. E.g., Mt. 5:21-44, 15:3-6, 21:12-13. So also Geisler, 1-3, 102.

8. E.g., Ex. 24:4, Josh. 1:7-8, 2 Chron. 34:14, Dan. 9:11, 13, Ezra 3:2, 6:18, 7:6; Mal. 4:4, Rom. 10:5 (see 2 Tim. 3:16; 2 Pet. 1:20-21; Jn. 10:35, 17:17)

9. See Motyer, "The Revelation of the Divine Name," 7-11; Currid, *Genesis*, 25, 29.

is a common case in which the preposition is to be borrowed from the preceding phrase. Motyer's translation of Exodus 6:3 is justified grammatically and captures the significance of the epochal shift at the Exodus:

> And I showed myself to Abraham, to Isaac, and to Jacob *in the character of* El Shaddai, but *in the character* expressed by my name Yahweh I did not make myself known to them.[10]

This translation is supported by the Exodus-like purpose statement in Jeremiah 16:21: "Therefore, behold, I will make them know, this once I will make them know my power and my might, and they shall know that my name is Yahweh." So many generations later, they clearly knew the sound of God's Name, but they needed to gain personal revelation of His character expressed by it.[11]

El Shaddai. In Hebrew, *El* is the singular form for "God." *Shaddai* means "enough."[12] He is the God who is enough. It is popularly translated "God Almighty." I think that unnecessarily limits the area of His self-sufficiency to power, when truly He has enough of everything He is. I would suggest "God All-sufficient." His power, though, is often emphasized contextually with this title, and the Greek translation carried into the New Testament is *pantokratōr*, "Almighty."[13] It is one of six elaborations of the title *El* in Genesis. The practice of compounding this designation for God after key events confirms that God's people were concerned with the character of God revealed through His working in history. After surveying the usage, Motyer provides a helpful summary:

> El Shaddai, then, is, first of all, the God who takes over human incapacity and transforms it. But also there is a consistency of suggestion as to the method of His working. The three patriarchs are either named or renamed by El Shaddai. El Shaddai,

---

10. "The Revelation of the Divine Name," 12.

11. *Ibid.*, 16-17.

12. Victor P. Hamilton, *TWOT*, 907.

13. E.g., Rev. 4:8, 11:17, 15:3; cf. Job 37:23 (Piper, "I Am Who I Am").

therefore, performs His wonders on the basis of a miracle worked on the individuals primarily concerned; the transformed human situation is a by-product of a transformed human nature. The third consistent feature of the revelation of El Shaddai is that He covenants to the patriarchs boundless posterity and inheritance of the land of promise. This is in accord with the previous two points: it was the claim of El Shaddai to be powerful where man was weakest, and He exerts this claim supremely by promising to an obscure and numerically tiny family that they should one day possess and populate a land which, in their day, was inhabited and owned by people immeasurably their superiors in number and power.[14]

That is the character in which God showed Himself to Abraham, Isaac, and Jacob. According to Exodus 6:2-3, there is additional, unique revelation of God's character in the Name Yahweh, not revealed to the patriarchs, but saved for the Exodus. Nevertheless, Motyer brilliantly points out that this particular glory of Yahweh could not be completely hidden in Genesis; one ray of light beamed forth and resulted in the only time the Name *Yahweh* was compounded like *El* so often was.[15] Significantly, for our study, that event also foreshadowed the Exodus, when Yahweh's character would be more fully revealed.

After God fulfilled His promise to miraculously create an heir in Sarah's dead womb, He tested Abraham by commanding him to sacrifice this one-of-a-kind son, Isaac (Gen. 22:1-2). But Yahweh had promised that Isaac would continue Abraham's line, inherit the land, and all the peoples of the earth would be blessed through him.[16] How could that happen if Abraham slew him? Abraham reckoned that God would resurrect Isaac in order to fulfill His promise (Heb. 11:17-19). "On the third day," Abraham told his servants, "I and the boy will go over there and worship and come again to you" (Gen. 22:5). Abraham believed that he would slay

---

14. "The Revelation of the Divine Name," 29-30.

15. *Ibid.*, 30.

16. Gen. 12:3, 17:19, 18:18, 21:12 (cf. 22:18)

Isaac, God would resurrect him, and they both would come back down mountain to meet the servants!

Isaac wondered why they were not taking a lamb up the mountain (22:7). Abraham responded in faith, "God will provide for himself the lamb," literally, "God will *see to* the lamb" (22:8). This literal usage continues in our idiom: when asked if we will have enough provisions, one may answer, "I'll *see to it*." (Through the Latin translation of this verse, we derive the theological term, the *Providence* of God. It conveys not only foresight of needs, but also the promise of pre-planning and working to meet those needs.)

Knowing God had chosen Isaac as the lamb for this burnt offering, Abraham placed Isaac on the altar and took out his knife to slaughter him. But Yahweh called from heaven to stop him. He affirmed Abraham's reverence for God, proven in the obedience of faith. Then Abraham looked and saw a ram that God had trapped in the thicket as a substitute for Isaac (22:13). "So Abraham called the name of that place, 'Yahweh-yireh'" (22:14), meaning, "Yahweh-Will-Provide," or more literally, "Yahweh-Will-See-To-It." Though the patriarchs often compounded the title *El*, this is the only time the Name Yahweh was elaborated by them. Through this foreshadow of the Exodus, *Yahweh showed Himself to Abraham as the One who providentially redeems through judgment upon His substitutionary sacrifice.*

THE EXODUS

The redemption of Isaac pointed to the future, fuller revelation of Yahweh's glory on a national scale. Yahweh's answer to Moses' complaint continued:

> EXODUS 6:2-8 (LIT.)
> God spoke to Moses and said to him, "*I am Yahweh*. ³I showed Myself to Abraham, to Isaac, and to Jacob, in the character of El Shaddai, but in the character of *My Name Yahweh* I did not

make Myself known to them. [4]I also established My covenant with them to give them the land of Canaan, the land in which they lived as sojourners. [5]Moreover, I have heard the groaning of the people of Israel whom the Egyptians hold as slaves, and I have remembered My covenant. [6]Say therefore to the people of Israel, '*I am Yahweh*, and I will bring you out from under the burdens of the Egyptians, and I will *deliver* you from slavery to them, and I will *redeem* you with an outstretched arm and with great acts of *judgment*. [7]I will take you to be My people, and I will be your God, and *you will know that I am Yahweh* your God, who has brought you out from under the burdens of the Egyptians. [8]I will bring you into the land that I swore to give to Abraham, to Isaac, and to Jacob. I will give it to you for a possession. *I am Yahweh*.'"

Four times in this short span, God declared, "I am Yahweh." Clearly, He purposed the "great acts" of the Exodus as a revelation of His glory to be known in His Name. Afterward, He favored the introduction, "I am Yahweh your God *who brought you out of Egypt*."[17] Later Scriptures attest that, through the Exodus, God "made a Name for" Himself.[18] That is to say, this event added meaning to the Name Yahweh and spread that significance far and wide.[19] We saw from Exodus 3:14-15 the aseity and sovereignty of God inherent in His Name, explained as, "I AM who I AM." *In Exodus 6:1-8, we see His Name is to be memorialized as the One who puts His self-sufficient sovereignty to work in redeeming His people through judgment and fulfilling His covenant promises.*

Through the plagues of Exodus, Yahweh demonstrated His sovereignty over all of creation. Not only did Yahweh cause creation to do His will, but He also controlled exactly when and where the plagues struck – against the Egyptians while protecting the Israelites in Goshen.[20] Have you ever wondered why God chose the specific plagues? Why turn the Nile to blood? Why frogs? Why

---

17. E.g., Ex. 20:2, Lev. 26:13, Ps. 81:10

18. Neh. 9:10, Jer. 32:20, Dan. 9:15

19. See *Part One*, 24-30, esp. pp. 29-30 on Ex. 18:9-11, Josh. 2:9-11, and Isa. 63:12, 14.

locusts? Yahweh was targeting all of the areas of the Egyptian gods' "power" to prove they were false and futile. I have detailed each plague elsewhere,[21] but for one example, the Egyptians sang hymns to a god named Hapi who (they believed) was in charge of the Nile and kept it alive and clean. Therefore, Yahweh proved that He Himself was in charge of the Nile, and Hapi was powerless to keep it or the Egyptians alive. One of the promised consequences of this plague was that the fish in the Nile would die (Ex. 7:18, 21). Yahweh thus judged the Egyptians' numerous fish deities, such as the goddess Hat-mehit. On the cusp of the final plague, God revealed this motive: "…and on all the gods of Egypt I will execute judgments: *I am Yahweh*" (Ex. 12:12, cf. Num. 33:4).

In order to multiply His wonders through ten plagues, Yahweh repeatedly strengthened Pharaoh's heart to refuse to let the Israelites go, even though his counselors advised him otherwise.[22] Among many false gods, the Egyptians believed that Re and Horus exercised absolute control over everything by means of their hearts. They also believed that the Pharaoh was an incarnation of these two gods; therefore, the Pharaoh controlled all things by means of his heart, empowered by the gods.[23] By repeatedly hardening Pharaoh's heart, Yahweh not only proved that Pharaoh did not control anything, but Yahweh also proved that He Himself controlled Pharaoh. As it is written, "Like, channels of, water is a, king's heart in the, hand of, Yahweh; He turns it wherever He pleases" (Prov. 21:1, AT). Yahweh did so with Pharaoh for the glory of His sovereignty expressed in His Name.[24]

---

20. Ex. 7:18; 8:4, 11, 21; 9:11, 14, cf. 8:22-23, 9:4-7, 9:26, 10:23, 11:7, 12:23

21. "Plagues on All the Egyptian gods" (ProjectOne28.com/plagues)

22. E.g., Ex. 4:21-23, 7:3-5, 10:7. I was first taught that God hardened Pharaoh's heart only after Pharaoh hardened his own heart. I now see that the Scriptural data is more complex than that – and it matters for the glory of Yahweh's Name. See "The Hardening of Pharaoh (and Millions of Others)" at ProjectOne28.com/hardening.

23. G. K. Beale, "An Exegetical and Theological Consideration of the Hardening of Pharaoh's Heart in Exodus 4-14 and Romans 9," *Trinity Journal* 5 NS (1984) 149 (see also his n. 84). Cf. John D. Currid, *Ancient Egypt and the Old Testament* (Grand Rapids, MI: Baker Books, 1997), 102-103.

Through the tenth and ultimate plague of the Exodus, Yahweh demonstrated the wrath and mercy that are core characteristics of His glory. Wrath is God's righteous response to rebellion against His infinite worth, born of His faithfulness to uphold His glory. The wages of sin is death under God's wrath,[25] and the Egyptians had sinned greatly against God, also brutalizing His people and murdering their baby boys. They deserved the vengeance of God.

At the beginning, Moses warned Pharaoh, "Thus says Yahweh, 'Israel is my firstborn son, and I say to you, "Let my son go that he may serve me." If you refuse to let him go, behold, I will kill your firstborn son'" (Ex. 4:22-23). After the repeated hardenings and repeated refusals to let Israel go, Moses announced that Yahweh would go through Egypt, and every firstborn son would die, from Pharaoh's to the least slave's, and also of the cattle (11:4-5). The Egyptians' god of life, Ptah, could do nothing to stop Yahweh.

> There shall be a great cry throughout all the land of Egypt, such as there has never been, nor ever will be again. [7]But not a dog shall growl against any of the people of Israel, either man or beast, that you may know that Yahweh makes a distinction between Egypt and Israel (11:6-7).

Why such a strange expression about no growling dog? Because the Egyptian god of the dead and embalming, Anubis, was depicted as a dog.[26] There was no real fight between Yahweh and the Egyptian gods; there would be no retaliation by Anubis to kill any Israelites. False gods are no gods and can do nothing to stop Yahweh: "See now that I, even I, am he, and there is no god beside me; I kill and I make alive; I wound and I heal; and there is none that can deliver out of my hand" (Deut. 32:39). The Egyptians learned this all too clearly. Ptah isn't. Anubis isn't. Yahweh *is* – the

---

24. Most pointedly, Ex. 9:16, "But for this purpose I have raised you up, to show you My power, so that My Name may be proclaimed in all the earth" (cf. 14:4, 17-18, Rom. 9:17). See also the lists in *Part One*, 26-27.

25. Rom. 6:23 (see "A Celebration of Propitiation" at ProjectOne28.com/propitiation)

26. Currid, *Ancient Egypt*, 113. This paragraph is taken from ProjectOne28.com/plagues.

I AM, the only God, sovereign over all things. And His wrath against sinners shows His glory.[27]

But what of the Israelites? Were they not also sinners? Did they not also deserve to die under God's wrath? Yes. But God had shown His glory by giving grace to Abraham, and now He would show the glory of His faithfulness in keeping His covenant with Abraham.[28] But God could not shrug off Israel's sinfulness. They denigrated His glory; if He did nothing, He, too, would denigrate His glory. In order to be holy and to show Israel that they also deserved wrath, Yahweh required Israel to be redeemed through the substitutionary sacrifice of the Passover lambs.

It is easy to mistake that the lamb saved only the firstborn Israelite sons. We must remember, though, that God considered the whole nation to be His firstborn son (4:22-23). Therefore, the lambs were substitutes for each member of the families; the lambs died in the place of all Israelites. To make this clear, God commanded that the households determine the size and number of lambs based upon the number of persons in their family, according to what each could eat (12:3-4). They were commanded to slaughter the lambs and spread the blood on the door frames, and then cook and eat them, each member of each family (12:7-8). Moses explained:

> "Yahweh will pass through to strike the Egyptians, and when he sees the blood on the lintel and on the two doorposts, Yahweh will pass over the door and will not allow the destroyer to enter your houses to strike you." ...And the people bowed their heads and worshiped (12:23, 27).

Through the tenth plague and Passover, Yahweh showed, more fully than ever before, the character of His Name: Yahweh alone is the self-sufficient sovereign, whose glory is His wrath and mercy, judgment and redemption. Yahweh also made this explicit in 33:18–34:7, which we analyzed in *Part One: Yahweh Himself*

---

27. Ex. 34:6-7. See "A Celebration of Propitiation" (ProjectOne28.com/propitiation).

defined His glory as His goodness known in His Name (as His reputation) for loving and judging, showing wrath against His enemies, and showing mercy by bearing iniquity for whom He freely chooses.[29]

This is so glorious, and yet it is only a foreshadow of greater glory to be revealed! Lambs cannot truly substitute for humans. They are not like us; we are worth far more (Mt. 12:12). The proper substitute would have to be human. Therefore, Isaiah prophesied about the Servant of Yahweh, a Branch from King David's family tree, a *human* who would be *"like a lamb,"* slaughtered to satisfy God's wrath against our sins![30]

But how could this be? How could one man absorb the infinite wrath of God toward so many people? Besides, every human is born a sinner in need of a redeemer. Every sinner can only die as punishment for his own sins, not as a substitute for the sins of others. No lamb *and no mere human* could volunteer, "I will lay down my *perfectly* obedient human life in the stead of these humans! Father, forgive them!" As they sang in Psalm 49:

> [7]Truly *no man can ransom another,*
>   or give to God the price of his life,
> [8]for the ransom of their life is costly
>   and can never suffice,
> [9]that he should live on forever
>   and never see the pit....
> [15]But *God will ransom my soul* from the power of Sheol,
>   for he will receive me.   *Selah*

The only way we could be ransomed by a perfect human substitute is if Yahweh became a perfect God-Man to bear His infinite wrath against us in His infinite Self. Fortunately for us,

---

28. Note the "steadfast love and faithfulness" in His definition of His glory known in His Name (Ex. 34:6, in answer to 33:18-19). Cf. Ex. 2:23-24, 6:5, 15:13; Dt. 4:37.

29. *Part One,* 9-10 (also n. 16), 54-56 (fulfillment in Christ). The addition of "whom He freely chooses" was developed through the *idem per idem* teaching here, pp. 11-13.

30. Isa. 11:1, 53:7. See pp. 86-89, to be unpacked in *Part Five, The Servant* (Lord willing).

that is the glory of His Name. And during the reign of Tiberius Caesar, a Man born in Bethlehem and raised in Galilee suddenly claimed to be Yahweh, here to save.

CHAPTER FOUR

JESUS IS THE I AM

Jesus of Nazareth was a Man. He touched, ate, drank, grew tired, slept, and when crucified, bled and died like the other humans beside Him.[1] Jesus called Himself "a Man" (Jn. 8:40). There is no record of any of His contemporaries denying His humanity. His opponents called Him a man (Jn. 10:33), and so did His supporters (e.g., Acts 2:22).

The curious tension arose because Jesus claimed to be more than a mere man. He spoke and acted like He was God the Son, in an eternal, co-equal, uniquely intimate relationship with God, His Father. In a context we will save for study in *Part Three, The Son of God and Son of Man*, the apostle John reported that, early in Jesus' ministry, "the Jews were seeking even more to kill Him, because not only was He breaking the Sabbath, but He also was calling God His own Father, making Himself equal with God" (5:18, AT). Later we will examine the more "subtle" ways He "made Himself equal with God," which will greatly enhance our appreciation of

---

1. E.g., Mk. 1:41, 2:16; Mt. 4:2, 8:24, 21:18, Jn. 4:6-7, 19:28; Lk. 22:44, Jn. 19:33-34

His character. But we might as well begin with the most blatant claims.

Before Abraham

In John 7-8, at the Feast of Tabernacles, the Jewish authorities sent guards to arrest Jesus while He was evangelizing the crowds in the temple. The guards decided not to. Interrogated, they responded, "A man never spoke like this" (7:46, AT). As Jesus preached before the Jewish leaders, many of them "believed" in Him, though this was clearly a superficial faith.[2] Therefore, Jesus said to them, "If you abide in my word, you are truly my disciples, and you will know the truth, and the truth will set you free" (8:31-32). This struck at their national pride, so they responded, "We are seed of Abraham, and we have served as slaves to no one – ever! How are you yourself saying that we will become free?" (8:33, AT). Obviously, they were subject to the Romans at the time, so they must have considered Jesus to be speaking of spiritual freedom.[3] As physical heirs of the promises of God given to Abraham, stewards of the Law given to Moses, they thought they were spiritually free. "Jesus answered them, 'Amen, amen, I am saying to you: everyone doing sin is a slave of sin…. Therefore, if the Son sets you free, you really will be free'" (8:34, 36, AT). Jesus explained they were not spiritually free, because they were sinners.

The conversation went downhill from there. Jesus claimed they were actually children of the devil, not Abraham (8:38, 41, 44). Jesus told the most respected spiritual authorities of the people of God that they did not belong to God (8:47). Therefore, the Jewish leaders called Jesus demon-possessed (8:48). He denied it and claimed that anyone who keeps His word will have eternal life

---

2. Cf. 8:31, 45. This theme is set up in 2:23–3:1. See D. A. Carson, *The Gospel according to John* (Grand Rapids, MI: Eerdmans, 1991), 184, 346-347; John Piper, "He Knew What Was In Man," 11 Jan 2009 (desiringGod.org/sermons/he-knew-what-was-in-man), and "The Truth Will Set You Free," 19 Mar 2011 (desiringGod.org/sermons/the-truth-will-set-you-free).

3. Cf. Carson, *John*, 349.

(8:49-51). Then the Jews retorted that Jesus boasted incredulously, since He is not greater than their "father," Abraham. Jesus admitted that He is actually greater than Abraham, so much so that:

> JOHN 8:56-58 (AT)
> "Abraham, 'your father,' experienced jubilation that he should see My day, and he saw it, and rejoiced." [57]Therefore, the Jews said to Him, "You do not yet have fifty years, and you have seen Abraham?" [58]Jesus said to them, "Amen, amen, I am saying to you: before Abraham was born, I AM."

Here, Jesus did not use proper grammar for the past tense context. He did not say, "Before Abraham was born, *I was.*" That would have been incredible enough, claiming to be preexistent (in existence before coming to earth), either as God or an angel or some other being. But Jesus did not ambiguously leave those other options open. He used the emphatic Greek, *"Egō eimi!"* By itself, *eimi* means, "I am." *Egō* means, "I," a purposeful redundancy: "I, I am!" Without doubt, Jesus used this emphatic combination because it was the official Greek translation of Yahweh's explanation of His Name in Exodus 3:14.[4] *Jesus declared that He existed before Abraham because He is Yahweh. Jesus declared Himself, now a Man, still to be the eternal, uncreated, unchanging, self-sufficient, sovereign Redeemer, the God of Israel.*

We find support for this obvious interpretation in the Jewish response: "Therefore, they took up stones in order that they might throw them at Him. But Jesus was hidden, and He went out of the temple" (8:59, AT). The Jews understood the reference to Exodus 3:14. They understood that Jesus' claim to be Yahweh was blatant blasphemy (unless, of course, it is true).

---

4. The LXX translated "I AM WHO I AM" as *egō eimi ho ōn* ("I AM the One who Is"). Some demur because *egō eimi* is reported on the lips of the formerly blind man (Jn. 9:9), but the contextual usage by Jesus (and the responses!) clearly put it in a category of its own. Some tie the allusion, not to Ex. 3:14, but to Isa. 41:4, 43:10, 13, 25; 46:4; 48:12 (*'anî hû'* in the Hb.; *egō eimi* in the LXX; e.g., Carson, *John*, 343, 358). I find this odd because Yahweh's statements through Isaiah are themselves allusions to Ex. 3:14! Cf. J. Alec Motyer, *The Prophecy of Isaiah: An Introduction & Commentary*

John 8:58 is probably the clearest of Jesus' many "I AM" statements in *The Gospel according to John*. Seven are followed by metaphorical predicates (metaphors that point to very real spiritual realities). Others are labeled absolute, meaning the "I AM" stands alone with no predicate after it, like John 8:58. Unfortunately, most modern English translations obscure these glorious statements, which we will clarify in this section for the sake of worship.

WALKING ON WATER

In John 6, Jesus fed upwards of 20,000 people with five loaves and two fish.[5] His twelve apostles even gathered twelve baskets full of leftovers (6:13). It was a New-Moses-for-a-New-Exodus-and-manna kind of miracle, just like the prophets had promised.[6] The crowd was ready to make Jesus king by force (6:15). Therefore, Jesus sent His disciples down to the Sea to sail across, while He dismissed the crowd and withdrew to a mountain alone.[7] Their idea of His kingship was not God's timing or God's way.

> And when evening came, His disciples went down to the sea, [17]and having embarked into a boat, they started across the sea to Capernaum, and it had become dark already, and Jesus had not yet come to them, [18]and the sea, because of a great wind blowing, was rising. [19]Then, having driven about twenty-five or thirty stadia, they are beholding Jesus walking upon the sea and coming near the boat, and they were afraid (6:16-19, AT).

Typically, humans do not walk on water. But Jesus walked on water! For three to four miles! The Greek behind "walking upon the sea" echoes Job 9:8 (LXX), which celebrates that God "alone" does such a thing. Jesus here did what only God does. He is not a second god, but God Himself, in flesh.

(Downers Grove, IL: IVP Academic, 1993), 334; Grant R. Osborne, *The Gospel of John* (Carol Stream, IL: Tyndale House, 2007), 95.

5.   Jn. 6:9-10, cf. Mt. 14:21, "about five thousand men, *besides women and children.*"

6.   Ex. 16, Dt. 18:15-19, Jn. 6:14, "the Prophet" (see ProjectOne28.com/two-testaments)

7.   Jn. 6:15, cf. Mt. 14:22-23, Mk. 6:45-46

Liberal critics often try to assert that Jesus did not claim to be God, nor did Matthew, Mark, or Luke portray Jesus as God, but the church later mythologized what we read in John, the last Gospel written. This is false for so many reasons,[8] one of which is this water-walking miracle, recorded by both Mark and Matthew. Mark 6:48 also reads that Jesus "came to them, walking on the sea" with the same Greek as Job 9:8 (LXX). Mark includes the additional phrase, "He meant to pass them by," with Greek echoing Job 9:11 (LXX), spoken about the God who *alone* stretched out the heavens, made the stars, does miracles beyond our comprehension, and exercises sovereignty that cannot be thwarted. *Jesus is the God of Job 9 – in flesh.*

Mark informs us that the disciples were afraid and cried out because they thought He was a ghost (6:49-50). Therefore, Jesus answered them with an emphatic claim to be Yahweh, not a ghost. Matthew and Mark share the same Greek as John 6:20 (AT) in the core statement:

> But He is saying ,to, them, "I AM; do not be fearing."

Sadly, most modern English translations render, "It is I." That is not what Jesus said. He said the same *egō eimi* as in John 8:58. The context also makes clear that this is no simple human identification. While demonstrating that He is Yahweh by treading upon the waves of the sea, Jesus also identified Himself as Yahweh, the I AM, sovereign over the wildest elements of His creation.[9] And when He entered the boat, the storm stilled (Mk. 6:51).

What is more, we again learn from the response to Jesus' audacity, this time from those with true, budding faith. Matthew (one of the early Gospel writers, whom the critics misinterpret) closes his report with, "And those in the boat worshiped him, saying,

---

8. See Chapter Six and also Simon Gathercole, *The Preexistent Son: Recovering the Christologies of Matthew, Mark, and Luke* (Grand Rapids, MI: Eerdmans, 2006).

9. See *Light Shines in the Darkness* for more on the significance of treading upon the unruly sea (free at ProjectOne28.com).

'Truly you are the Son of God'" (14:33). They *worshiped* Him! This group of Jewish monotheists, who sincerely believed the One true God named Yahweh was alone worthy of worship – these Jews worshiped a Jewish Man! They believed Jesus' demonstration and proclamation to be Yahweh. They were not flippantly apostatizing from their deeply held monotheism; they were not adding Jesus as a second god. They believed He is "the Son of God," in perfect Oneness with God the Father. So they gave Him the worship due to the only God. And so should we!

Seven "I Am" Metaphors

Bread of Life. When Jesus and the Twelve reached the other side, they were met by a hungry crowd that was stalking the bread-multiplier. They were curious about how Jesus traveled, since they knew He did not get in the boat with the disciples, but Jesus did not answer that question (Jn. 6:22-25). Instead, He indicted their priority for temporary food, rather than eternal life, which He could give them if they truly believed (6:26-29). In response, they demanded a heavenly sign, like the manna from heaven (6:30-31). In the ensuing dialogue, Jesus repeated a similar statement three times: "I AM the bread of life" (6:35), "I AM the bread of life" (6:48), and, "I AM the living bread" (6:51).

This is the first of Jesus' seven metaphors in *The Gospel according to John* that are preceded by the emphatic *egō eimi*, alluding to the Name Yahweh. We classify them as metaphors because Jesus is not literally bread, nor a gate, nor a vine; literally, He is the God-Man. Nevertheless, metaphors communicate truths by correlating some fact belonging to the symbol with the spiritual reality of the referent. In this case, the symbol is bread, which gives sustenance. The referent is Jesus, and the spiritual reality of the metaphor is that Jesus is the eternal life-giver.

With this first metaphor, Jesus explained that the manna in Exodus 16 was a parable of His incarnation and salvation.

Originally, the manna fell from heaven to save the Israelites' physical lives during the wilderness wanderings. That pointed to the ultimate reality: Jesus *coming down from heaven* and giving eternal life to the world (6:33). By this, Jesus claimed that He did not begin to exist in Mary's womb. Before Jesus was Mary's Baby, He was Mary's Creator. He was the I AM in heaven, and He voluntarily chose to come down to earth, becoming the God-Man, to give His uncreated life to the world.

Jesus had multiplied bread the day before, but He does not merely give bread; He gives Himself – better than that which feeds the body, is digested, and leaves us hungry again. He said, "I AM the bread of life; the one, *coming* to Me absolutely, cannot hunger, and the one, *believing* into Me absolutely, will not thirst – ever!" (6:35, AT). Based upon the parallel structure, we can define saving *faith* as *coming* to Jesus for eternal satisfaction.[10] Because Jesus is Yahweh, He is the all-sufficient source of all goodness. Every hunger and thirst, every spiritual desire, can be filled to satisfaction by eating and drinking Jesus, getting Him in you, metabolizing Him so that He becomes your life. With Christ in you, you will never lack.

> JOHN 6:41-42 (AT)
> Therefore, the Jews were grumbling about Him because He said, "I AM the bread having come down from heaven," [42]and they were saying, "This is Jesus, the son of Joseph, is it, not? We ourselves know his, father and mother, do we, not? How now is he saying that he has come down from heaven?"

The vast majority of the crowd could not see past His humanity to believe in His deity. But this is precisely what we must do. Jesus taught about their spiritual inability and utter need for God's gracious drawing and teaching and giving the ability to come to

---

10. Cf. Jn. 4:14, 7:37-39; John Piper, *Future Grace: The Purifying Power of the Promises of God*, Revised Edition (Colorado Springs: Multnomah Books, 2012), 205, 214; also, "Behold, Believe, Be Raised," 22 Nov 2009 (desiringGod.org/sermons/behold-believe-be-raised).

Him.[11] Jesus claimed, "...and indeed, the bread which I Myself will give on behalf of the life of the world is My flesh" (6:51, AT). They quarreled with each other about how that could work (6:52). I doubt they thought Jesus was suicidally advocating cannibalism; they were accustomed to metaphors and spiritual analogies in the Hebrew Scriptures, though they surely thought this one was tasteless.[12] Jesus did not back down, but continued to teach that, since we are born spiritually dead in sin, if we do not receive Jesus as the I AM, then we do not have spiritual life (6:53). Remember that eating Christ's flesh and drinking His blood symbolize believing into Him, as is clear in His parallel statements in 6:35. Jesus pointed to His giving up His flesh and blood through His substitutionary death on the Cross. If we believe, He will come into us like bread enlivens a body.

But how could a mere man make his life become eternal life in us? Nearly all left after this difficult teaching (6:66). Only eleven disciples believed that He was more than a mere man, because of God's gracious choice.[13] If you are struggling to believe, do not put any trust in your natural self, which benefits nothing,[14] but cry out in prayer to God for Him to overcome your sinful inability and give you the ability to see Jesus as the I AM, the bread of life, so that you come to Him to be satisfied with all that Yahweh is for you in Christ.[15] If you have believed, do not boast, but praise the glory of His grace, by which He drew you to Himself.[16]

Light of the World. The Feast of Tabernacles celebrated the gracious presence of God with the Exodus generation, protecting them and sustaining them in the wilderness.[17] They had followed

---

11. Jn. 6:36-37, 44-45, cf. 6:63, 64, 65, 70; the Twelve minus Judas (6:64, 70-71)

12. Cf. Carson, *John*, 295-296.

13. Jn. 6:67-69, esp. 6:70, cf. Mt. 11: 25-27, 16:16-17 and footnote 11 above.

14. Jn. 6:63

15. See footnote 11 above.

16. 1 Cor. 1:29-31; Eph. 1:6, 2:8-10, and footnotes 11 and 13, above.

17. Lev. 23:33-44

the glory cloud by day and the pillar of fire by night. When Yahweh stopped, the Israelites stopped and camped in tabernacles (tents) around the Tabernacle, filled with the glory of Yahweh.[18] Therefore, each year during this festival, the Israelites lived in tents outside of their villages, celebrating the original Exodus and hoping for the promised New Exodus, deliverance from their new enemies and the inauguration of the kingdom of God on a new earth.[19] Symbolic of Yahweh's fiery presence during the Exodus, they lit four huge lamps in the temple court. D. A. Carson explains the background rituals:

> 'Men of piety and good works' danced through the night, holding burning torches in their hands and singing songs and praises. The Levitical orchestras cut loose, and some sources attest that this went on every night of the Feast of Tabernacles, with the light from the temple area shedding its glow all over Jerusalem.[20]

In this context,[21] Jesus proclaimed, "I AM the light of the world! The one, following *Me* absolutely, cannot walk in the darkness, but he will have the light of life" (8:12, AT). Once again Jesus claimed to be Yahweh, the One of whom David sang, "Yahweh is my light and my salvation" (Ps. 27:1), the One of whom Isaiah prophesied, in a New Exodus context: "Yahweh will be your everlasting light," replacing the sun and moon (60:19, 20).[22] At this festival, Jesus of Nazareth claimed to be the light of Genesis 1:3 (which preceded the sun[23]), the light of the Exodus, and the light of the New Creation – *Yahweh*.

Jesus also promised that His disciples will possess "the light of life" (Jn. 8:12). The light signifies revelation of His glory and the

---

18. Ex. 13:22-23, 14:19, 24; 40:34-38; Num. 2:1-2

19. See "Tying the Two Testaments Together" (ProjectOne28.com/two-testaments).

20. *John*, 337.

21. Jn. 7:53–8:11 was not part of John's original Greek Gospel, so the Feast setting of 7:2, 14, and 37 is still the setting in 8:12 (see ProjectOne28.com/john/adultery-pericope).

22. Cf. Zech. 14:6-9 (alluded to in Jn. 7:38, same festival). Fulfillment: Rev. 21:23, 22:5.

resulting purity that overcomes sinful works of darkness by His grace.[24] This light is "of life," that is, it comes from the life – the life produces it (cf. Jn. 1:4). No life, no light. Dead people cannot see. Without the light of life, we cannot even see the kingdom of God for what it is (3:3). Without the life, we hate the light and refuse to come to it, preferring our evil deeds (3:19-20). Jesus is life, and He is light. When His life comes into you, by His Spirit, His life gives light to see Him as He is and to be transformed into His image. The light of life shows us that Jesus is Yahweh in flesh, our Creator and Redeemer. Such gracious light!

Gate and Good Shepherd. Jesus said, "I AM the gate for the sheep.... I AM the gate, if anyone comes through *Me*, he will be saved, and he will come in, and he will go out, and he will find pasture.... I Myself have come that they may have life and have it abundantly" (Jn. 10:7, 9, 10, AT). What a bold claim to be the One who determines which sheep belong in the flock (God's people), the One who gives life, protects, and nourishes them.[25] Surely this prerogative and ability belong only to Yahweh,[26] which is Jesus' point: He is the I AM.

Quickly shifting metaphors, Jesus said, "I AM the good shepherd.... I AM the good shepherd, and I know the sheep which are Mine..." (10:11, 14, AT). Jesus here asserted ownership of the people of God, explicitly ("Mine") and implicitly ("good shepherd" or "noble shepherd"[27]). The background for this metaphor is Ezekiel 34, when Yahweh indicted the bad shepherds of Israel during the exile and promised His personal response:

---

23. The sun was not made until Day Four (Gen. 1:14-19).

24. Jn. 1:4, 5, 9, 3:19-21; cf. Carson, *John*, 119, 207-208; John Piper, "I Am the Light of the World" (desiringGod.org/sermons/i-am-the-light-of-the-world).

25. Going out and coming in echoes language of life in covenant with God (Deut. 28:6), life which Yahweh (Jesus) oversees (Ps. 121:8).

26. "The Lord knows who are his" (2 Tim. 2:19, echoing Num. 16:5 of Yahweh, cf. Nah. 1:7).

27. As Carson suggests (*John*, 386).

> "For thus says the Lord Yahweh: Behold, I, I myself will search
> for my sheep and will seek them out. [12]As a shepherd seeks out
> his flock when he is among his sheep that have been scattered,
> so will I seek out my sheep, and I will rescue them from all
> places where they have been scattered.... [15]*I myself will be the
> shepherd of my sheep*, and I myself will make them lie down,
> declares the Lord Yahweh. [16]I will seek the lost, and I will bring
> back the strayed,[28] and I will bind up the injured, and I will
> strengthen the weak.... [22]I will rescue my flock.... [23]And I will
> set up over them one shepherd, my servant David, and he shall
> feed them: he shall feed them and be their shepherd. [24]And
> I, Yahweh, will be their God, and my servant David shall be
> prince among them. I am Yahweh; I have spoken" (Ezek. 34:11-
> 12, 15-16, 22-24).

In that fascinating prophecy, Yahweh promised to be the good
shepherd who saves His people from the dire consequences of their
bad shepherds, and He also promised to put over them a human
shepherd, "David." This does not mean the literal David, raised
from the dead. It is similar to the promise that "Elijah" would
precede the coming of the Lord, which was fulfilled in John
the Baptist, who came "in the spirit and power of Elijah."[29] The
Israelites all knew that the Messiah would be the *Son of* David.[30]
Well, "like father, like son." The ultimate Son of David would
be so much *like David* that the prophets sometimes called him
David.[31] So, in Ezekiel 34, Yahweh will become their shepherd,
and the Son of David will become their shepherd. Little did they
know the same Person would fulfill both aspects of this promise!
By proclaiming, "*Egō eimi* the good shepherd," Jesus identified
Himself as Yahweh; by speaking it as a Man, Jesus was the Davidic
Messiah – two natures in One Person, the God-Man!

Still more dramatic, the God-Man said, "The good shepherd
lays down his soul for his sheep" when he sees the wolf coming

---

28. Cf. Lk. 19:10, 15:4, Mt. 15:24, 18:12.

29. Mal. 4:5, Lk. 1:17, Mt. 11:14, Mk. 9:13

30. 2 Sam. 7:12-17; cf. Mt. 22:41-42

(10:11 and context). And, "I lay down My soul for the sheep" (10:15, AT). Carson teaches "the assumption is that the sheep are in mortal danger; that in their defence the shepherd loses his life; that by his death they are saved."[32] The sheep deserved to be slaughtered for their sins, but Yahweh-become-flesh would voluntarily lay down His soul "for" the sheep, that is, in their stead and for their sake, a substitutionary sacrifice. A dead shepherd would expose the flock to greater danger, if He was not also the next I AM metaphor.

Resurrection and Life. Toward the end of Jesus' ministry, one of His best friends became deathly ill while Jesus was far away. Having received the news, Jesus said, "This sickness is not unto death, but for the glory of God, in order that the Son of God may be glorified through it" (11:4, AT). The next words surprise:

> And Jesus *was loving* Martha and her sister and Lazarus. [6] *Therefore*, when He heard, "He is sick," He then indeed abided in the place in which He was for two days... (11:5-6, AT).

Because Jesus was loving them, He delayed! *Because* He was loving them, He allowed Lazarus to suffer and die. Jesus' love for Lazarus would be repeatedly questioned by Martha, Mary, and the crowd[33] because He let him die. How is that loving? Because love seeks the best for the objects of its love. In this instance, health and life were not best. What could be better? Seeing and believing and delighting in the glory of God's Son. Jesus explained this to His disciples: "Lazarus died, and I am rejoicing on account of you, *in order that you may believe*, because I was not there, but let us go to him" (11:14-15, AT).

When Jesus finally arrived, Martha let out her grief in the mild indictment, "Lord, if You were here, my brother would not have died" (11:21, AT). Truly, it was not necessary that Jesus be present;

---

31. Jer. 30:9, Ezek. 34:23, 37:24, Hos. 3:5

32. *John*, 386.

33. Jn. 11:21, 32, 37

He could have healed Lazarus from afar, like the official's son (4:46-54). But Jesus wanted this interaction with Martha: "Jesus is saying to her, 'Your brother will resurrect.' 24Martha is saying to Him, 'I know that he will resurrect at the resurrection on the last day'" (11:23-24, AT). Martha possessed the right doctrine based on the Hebrew Scriptures. But Jesus shifted her solid theology into focused faith:

> "I AM the resurrection and the life; the one believing into *Me*, even if he dies, he will live, 26and everyone living and believing into *Me* absolutely cannot die into the age to come. Are you believing this?" (11:25-26, AT).

Again, who can claim to be the object of saving faith and the source of resurrection life, except Yahweh, the I AM WHO I AM? Jesus is He! Martha modeled the right response for us: "Yes, Lord, I myself have believed that You Yourself are the Christ, the Son of God, the One coming into the world!" (11:27, AT).

But Martha then doubted the wisdom of Jesus' command to open her brother's tomb four days after his death. Jesus gave her a kind rebuke: "I told you that, if you believe, you will see the glory of God, did I not?"[34] Then God the Word (1:1), who spoke all things into existence (1:3), "called out with a great voice, 'Lazarus, come out!'" (11:43, AT). Let us be real: dead people cannot obey commands. But, just like our loud voices can wake those who are sleeping, Jesus' call is effectual even for the dead. His call effects what it wills, causing it to come into being. As the all-powerful Creator, Jesus' words create what they command. His word gave Lazarus the ability to "come out" of the grave. And by it, we see the glory of God (11:40), the manifestation of Yahweh in flesh.

The Way, the Truth, and the Life. On the night before Judas' betrayal, Jesus spoke of His departure back to where He came from, the Father in heaven (Jn. 13:33–14:4). Thomas was distressed, but Jesus reassured:

"I AM the way and the truth and the life; no one comes to the Father except through *Me*. [7]If you ,all, have known Me, you will know My Father also. And from now, you know Him, and you have seen Him." [8]Philip is saying ,to, Him, "Lord, show us the Father, and it is enough ,for, us." [9]Jesus is saying ,to, him, "So much time I am with you ,all,, and you, Philip, have not known Me? The ,one, having seen *Me* has seen the Father; how are you yourself saying, 'Show us the Father'? [10]You are believing that I ,am, in the Father, and the Father is in *Me*, ,are you, not?" (14:6-10, AT).

The religious pluralism of our age, which asserts that all religions are equally valid because there are many paths to God, is a lie from hell. The only way to right relationship with God in His joyful presence is through His Son, Jesus Christ, who is the way and the truth. Truth is what corresponds to reality. Jesus is ultimate reality, the I AM; every real thing gets its realness from Him, the uncreated Life who creates and sustains all things. In Him we have our being.[35] Apart from Him we are nothing and receive nothing. To see Him is to see God the Father. The fullness of Godhood dwells bodily in Jesus (Col. 2:9, 1:19). He is the manifest Glory of God (Jn. 1:14, 18; Heb. 1:3). Let us believe and marvel!

The True Vine. Jesus taught, "I AM the true vine, and My Father is the vinedresser.... I AM the vine; you ,are, the branches. The ,one, abiding in *Me* and I am in him, this ,one, is bearing much fruit because, apart from *Me*, you have power to be doing ,absolutely, nothing" (15:1, 5, AT). The Old Testament background is again essential. Psalm 80:8, in the context of the Exodus, sang of Israel as a vine that God took out of Egypt and planted in the Promised Land. But the vine was cut down in God's judgment (vv. 12-13, 16). In verse 15, the psalmist pleaded that God would have regard "for this vine... for the son whom you made strong for yourself." So, Israel was called God's vine and God's son. Therefore, Jesus

---

34. Jn. 11:40 (AT), asked with οὐκ ("not"), signaling the expectation of a positive answer.

35. Acts 17:28, cf. Jn. 1:3; 1 Cor. 8:6, Col. 1:15-17, Heb. 1:2-3.

here claimed to be the true Israel, the true vine and true Son of God. Jesus succeeded where Israel failed – obedient in temptation, a faithful priest, advancing the kingdom of God.[36]

Therefore, Jesus is the true vine to whom everyone must be connected for life and inclusion in the people of God. John Murray wrote, "Union with Christ is the central truth of the whole doctrine of salvation."[37] Through faith, we are united with Christ in His death, resurrection, ascension, session, and second coming. United with Christ, we receive regeneration, justification, adoption, perseverance, resurrection, and glorification.[38] This only makes sense if Jesus is Yahweh. David Wells gets it right: "To speak of being 'in' a teacher, and of participating at an ontological and ethical level in that teacher's capacities, would be preposterous if that teacher were not divine."[39] Robert Peterson adds clarity:

> It helps to understand this argument for Christ's deity by putting other beings in his place in the equation. What sense does it make to say that we are "in the archangel Michael" or that "we died, were buried, and raised with the apostle Peter"? To ask these absurd questions is to answer them. It makes no sense at all to say that we are spiritually joined to mere creatures, whether angelic or human. It is, to use Wells's apt word, *preposterous*. Why? Because Christ's place in saving union is surely the place that only God occupies! … Only union with God himself brings regeneration, justification, adoption, perseverance, resurrection, and glorification. Union with Christ, then, is a sweeping and powerful demonstration of our Lord's deity.[40]

---

36. For more, see "Introduction to the Old Testament" (ProjectOne28.com/OTsurvey).

37. *Redemption Accomplished and Applied* (Grand Rapids, MI: Eerdmans, 1995), 170, qtd. in Robert A. Peterson, "Toward a Systematic Theology of the Deity of Christ," in *The Deity of Christ*, ed. Christopher W. Morgan & Robert A. Peterson (Wheaton, IL: Crossway, 2011), 210.

38. Peterson, *op. cit.*, 209, 210.

39. *The Person of Christ: A Biblical and Historical Analysis of the Incarnation* (Wheaton, IL: Crossway, 1984), 61, qtd. in Peterson, 210.

40. Peterson, *op. cit.*, 210-211.

That You May Believe

At the last supper, Jesus told the future, the betrayal of Judas,[41] for a specific purpose: "I am saying this to you certainly before it happens, in order that, whenever it happens, you may believe that I AM" (13:19, AT). Who knows the future? Prophets? Only because they learn it from God. Yahweh had made clear, through Isaiah,[42] that it is proof of Godhood to declare the future and bring it to pass because only God knows everything about the future and reigns over it. Jesus explained that He did not foretell Judas' betrayal as a prophet, but as the I AM, Yahweh, who knows all things, even the future decisions of His creatures. He was not surprised by Judas' betrayal; He preordained it to precipitate the voluntary laying down of His soul for His sheep.[43]

They Fell to the Ground

Perhaps the most fascinating absolute I AM statement came at Jesus' arrest, when He met the soldiers:

> JOHN 18:4-6 (AT)
> Jesus, therefore, having known all the things, coming upon Him, came out and is saying to them, "Whom are you seeking?" [5]They answered Him, "Jesus, the Nazarene." He is saying to them, "I AM." ...[6]Therefore, *when He said to them, "I AM," they went backwards and fell to the ground!*

The soldiers did not hear a normal, "I am he," from a mere man.[44] In this moment Jesus released the power of His Person, the almighty Word that caused galaxies to spring into being (Jn. 1:1,

---

41. See the repeated emphasis on Jesus' omniscient foreknowledge in Jn. 13:1-3, 10-11, 18 (and sovereignty in Jn. 13:3, cf. 17:2, Mt. 11:27).

42. E.g., Isa. 41:23, 44:6-8, 46:8-11 (see ProjectOne28.com/open-theism)

43. Lk. 22:22, Jn. 17:12 (Acts 1:16), Acts 2:23, 4:27-28, cf. Jn. 10:11, 15, 17-18. Consider also Rev. 13:8, 17:8; 1 Pet. 1:20; 2 Tim. 1:9; Eph. 1:4-5, 11.

44. Carson's equivocation is bewildering (*John*, 578-79). They fell to the ground! In the words of Tim Lockwood (Flint's dad in *Cloudy with a Chance of Meatballs*), "That's not natural."

3). These soldiers had assumed strength with their weapons. They came to overpower Jesus. But the sheer force of a four-syllable revelation of His Name, *egō eimi*, knocked them backwards! This is the sovereign Creator; they will not seize Him against His will. Having demonstrated that vividly, Jesus asked them again whom they were seeking and offered Himself freely to be arrested and crucified, to drink the cup of God's wrath for our sins (18:7-11).

Jesus' *Egō Eimi* Sayings in *The Gospel according to John*	
6:20	walking upon the sea: "I AM! Do not afraid."
6:35, 48, 51	"I AM the bread of life." "I AM the living bread."
8:12, 9:5	"I AM the light of the world."
8:24	"...unless you believe that I AM, you will die in your sins."
8:28	"When you lift up Son of Man, then you will know that I AM...."
8:58	"Amen, amen... before Abraham was born, I AM."
10:7, 9	"I AM the gate for the sheep."
10:11, 14	"I AM the good shepherd."
11:25	"I AM the resurrection and the life."
13:19	asserting foreknowledge: "that you may believe... that I AM"
14:6	"I AM the way and the truth and the life."
15:1	"I AM the true vine."
18:5-6	"...when He said to them, 'I AM,' they... fell to the ground."

Unless You Believe

Since both the absolute I AM statements and the metaphors communicate the reality of Jesus' Godhood, we must believe them or perish. In another absolute statement, *Jesus said, "...unless you believe that I AM, you will die in your sins" (8:24, AT)*. Again, it is so sad that most modern English versions mistranslate, "Unless you believe that I am *he*." I am who? There is no referent in context. Both NIV and NLT fancifully supply, "Unless you believe that I am the one I claim to be"[45] or "who I claim to be." In fact, Jesus said, "Unless you believe that *egō eimi*," I AM![46] We must translate correctly and believe correctly. *We must believe, before we die, that Jesus is Yahweh in order to be saved from the eternal judgment we deserve for our sins.*

That is the meaning of His Name. *Yeshua* means *Yahweh saves.* The angel instructed, "You will call His Name *Yeshua* because *He Himself will save* His people from their sins" (Mt. 1:21, AT). Yahweh was not saving through a separate third party; *He Himself* was saving – Yahweh the Son, Yahweh-in-flesh. Receive Him. Be believing upon *His Name.*[47]

---

45. NIV 2011 amended without correcting: "I am he."

46. Remember the context: this contention leads to 8:58, "Before Abraham was born, I AM," followed by their attempted stoning for blasphemy (8:59). Cf. Carson, *John*, 343; Osborne, *John*, 131. Remember also the same construction in 13:19, "that you may believe that I AM," while asserting an attribute belonging only to Yahweh, foreknowledge.

47. Jn. 1:12, 3:18, 20:30-31; Acts 3:16, 4:12, 10:43; 1 Jn. 3:23, 5:13; Rev. 2:13

CHAPTER FIVE

JESUS AS GOD
IN THE OLD TESTAMENT

Jesus existed as God the Son for an eternity before becoming flesh.[1] He is, eternally, the Word, the Self-expression of God (Jn. 1:1). He is, eternally, the image and radiant glory of the unseen God.[2] Jesus is not only the God of the New Testament; Jesus is also the God of the Old Testament. No one has ever seen God the Father.[3] Therefore, every appearance of God in the Old Testament was a manifestation of the pre-infleshed Jesus, that is, the eternal Son of God before He became a Baby and was named Jesus. In this chapter, we will find the pre-incarnate Son alive and active in the Old Testament as God in relationship with God. We will

---

1. The case for this is made below.

2. Phil. 2:6, Col. 1:15; 2 Cor. 4:4; Heb. 1:3

3. Jn. 1:18, 5:37, 6:46; 1 Jn. 4:12; 1 Tim. 6:16; Col. 1:15. "This very line of argument is a central feature of Patristic exegesis..." (Günther Juncker, "Christ As Angel: The Reclamation of a Primitive Title," *Trinity Journal* 15:2 [Fall 1994], 249, n. 110). "All of the church fathers prior to Augustine attributed OT theophanies to the Son" (235). It may be that these verses teach only that no one has seen the *Triune* God *in His fullness*. I welcomed the correction by Andrew Malone of simplistic thinking about the "invisibility" of God (*Knowing Jesus in the Old Testament? A Fresh Look at Christophanies* [Nottingham, England: Inter-varsity, 2015]). It is not that God cannot be seen at

discover that He is the Messenger of Yahweh, who is Yahweh Himself. Then we will finish by highlighting certain prophecies that Yahweh would become a God-Man to reign forever on earth as the Messiah.

IN ISAIAH: THE KING, YAHWEH OF ARMIES

Isaiah 6 records the call of Isaiah and his commissioning as a prophet. He reported: "I saw the Lord [*Adonai*] sitting upon a throne, high and lifted up; and the train of his robe filled the temple" (6:1). The seraphim (literally, "burning ones," angels) dared not look at God, but covered their faces and called to one another (6:3, AT):

> Holy, holy, holy is Yahweh of armies;
> the whole earth is full of His glory!

Isaiah cried out in confessional fear that he would die, "because my eyes have seen the King, Yahweh of armies!" (6:5, AT). Isaiah saw Yahweh. No one has ever seen the Father. Therefore, Isaiah saw the pre-incarnate Son. So says John 12:41 (AT), after quoting one passage from Isaiah 6 and one from Isaiah 53: "These things Isaiah said because he saw His glory, and he spoke about Him," Jesus. Isaiah saw Jesus on His heavenly throne more than 700 years before He was born! Because Jesus is Yahweh!

Notably, in that same passage, Yahweh also spoke to Himself in the plural, "And I heard the voice of the Lord [*Adonai*], saying, 'Whom shall I send, and who will go for Us?'" (Isa. 6:8 NASB). Isaiah was commissioned on behalf of the Three-in-One God, having seen the glory of Yahweh the Son. The Trinity is not bluntly spelled out in the Old Testament, as it is in the New, just like many other teachings, because God chose to conceal and progressively

---

all, because we *will* see Him, the Father in all His glory, on the New Earth (e.g., Mt. 5:8, Rev. 22:4). However, my faith that the OT appearances of God were manifestations of God the Son is based on Biblical revelations of the Son's eternal role in the Trinity. So I was not persuaded by his arguments against my position here, shared by many noble teachers throughout history. For more, see ProjectOne28.com/christophanies.

reveal Himself throughout history (Prov. 25:2). Nevertheless, this plural nature of the One true God is a frequent hint, which began as quickly as it possibly could have.

IN GENESIS: THE SECOND PERSON OF THE TRIUNE GOD

We find the first hint of Jesus' eternal existence in the Bible's very first verse: "In the beginning, *Elohim* created…" (Gen. 1:1). *Elohim* is the plural form of the Hebrew *El* or *Eloah*, "God."[4] On this basis, Mormon founder Joseph Smith taught that it should translated "gods."[5] (This is but one of many reasons Mormonism should not be considered Christian.) Smith did not understand the Hebrew. When *Elohim* is paired with a plural verb, then it refers to false gods.[6] When *Elohim* is paired with a singular verb, it refers to the One true God.[7] English comparisons can help us grasp the need for noun-verb agreement:

> God is One.
> Gods is many.
> God are many.
> Gods are false.

The middle two examples are incorrect grammar. The first and last examples are correct because the singular noun agrees with the singular verb, and the plural noun matches the plural verb. The Hebrew Scriptures consistently break this norm when describing the action of the Three-in-One *Elohim* with a singular verb in order to distinguish Him from false gods.

Throughout the Creation account, we read, "And God *said….* And God *said….* And God *said….*" These are reports of God the Father creating through the agency of God the Son, who is *the*

---

4. See Jack Scott in n. 9 below.

5. E.g., *The Teachings of Joseph Smith* (Deseret Book Co., 1977), 370-372 (scriptures.byu. edu/tpjs/STPJS.pdf).

6. NASB translates *elohim* as "gods" over two hundred times (e.g., Ex. 20:3).

7. *TWOT*, 44.

Word (Jn. 1:1-3). When God "said," the creative power of His Son was released.

In Genesis 1:26, *Elohim* spoke to Himself in the plural,[8] "Let *Us* create Man in *Our* image, according to *Our* likeness" (AT). The Father, Son, and Holy Spirit in counsel – not three gods, but Three Persons in One God, with one image: "So God created man in *his* own image" (1:27). The image of God, in which we were created, is the uncreated Son of God (Col. 1:15-16), who was present in Genesis 1.

Some have categorized these examples (also Gen. 3:22, 11:7) as a "plural of majesty" or "plural of respect" (literary devices not to be taken literally). However:

> …no evidence exists that Moses or the prophets or any of the kings of Israel ever spoke in this manner. This has been pointed out by no less an authority than Gesenius, the father of all Hebrew lexicons: "The use of the plural as a form of respectful address is quite foreign to Hebrew…."[9]

It is better to understand this as Yahweh's hint that He is Three-in-One. Before becoming the God-Man, Jesus eternally co-existed as the Second Member of the Triune God.

Jesus is *Yahweh Elohim*, who, as the image of the unseen God, walked with Adam and Eve in the breeze of the day (Gen. 3:8). Jesus is the God who walked with Enoch and Noah (5:22-24, 6:8-9).

---

8. God also spoke of Himself in the plural in Gen. 3:22, 11:7. The typical Jewish teaching is that the One God is speaking to the heavenly council of angels (e.g., Nahum Sarna, *Genesis*, The JPS Torah Commentary [Philadelphia: The Jewish Publication Society, 1989], 12). But this cannot be, because we are not created in the image of angels. Tellingly, Sarna does not comment on the plurality of "in Our Image, in Our Likeness" (Gen. 1:26).

9. Anthony Rogers, "Let Us Make Man: A Trinitarian Interpretation" (answeringislam. org/authors/rogers/genesis_1_26_trinitarian.html), citing Gesenius, *Hebrew Grammar*, ed. E. Kautzsch, trans. A. E. Crowley (Oxford, 1976), 398. Cf. the uniqueness noted by Jack B. Scott: "More probable is the view that *'elōhîm* comes from *'elôah* as a unique development of the Hebrew Scriptures and represents chiefly the plurality of persons in the Trinity of the godhead" (*TWOT*, 41, cf. 44); "…the form *Elōhîm* occurs only in Hebrew and in no other Semitic language, not even in Biblical Aramaic" (44).

When Yahweh manifested to Abraham as a "Man," our forefather saw God the Son. That fascinating passage in Genesis 18 begins, "And Yahweh appeared to him…" (v. 1). When Abraham looked, "behold, three *men* were standing in front of him" (v. 2). Abraham bowed and asked his Adonai to stay for some bread (vv. 3-8). "They ate" (v. 8). How can Yahweh eat, and who are the other two "men"? Those two left to investigate and overthrow Sodom (vv. 16, 22) and are called "two angels" (19:1). Only two went to Sodom, "but Abraham still stood before Yahweh" (18:22). Abraham did not see God the Father; he saw God the Son imaging forth *like* a Man in something of a precursor to His true incarnation![10] This actually was a frequent occurrence in the Old Testament.

THE ANGEL OF YAHWEH

Exodus 3. We glossed over a significant detail in our Exodus 3 education of Yahweh's Name, in order to save it for here. When I was little, perhaps under the influence of felt board Sunday School teachings, I thought all Moses saw was a fiery bush, and God, who stayed in heaven, caused His voice to come out of the bush like a talented ventriloquist. I missed the introduction in verse 2: the Being whom Moses met in the burning bush was actually "the Angel of Yahweh." *The Angel of Yahweh is Yahweh Himself.*[11] We will see the Scriptures repeatedly and explicitly make this identification. But first, we should remove a stumbling block. We easily hang up on the word *angel* because we think it can only mean a specific kind of *creature*. However, the Hebrew and Greek for "angel" means "messenger."[12] It is often used of human

---

10. Recall Ezekiel's heavenly vision, quoted in *Part One* (49-50): "seated above the likeness of a throne was a likeness with a human appearance" (1:26).

11. See Motyer, *Exodus*, 50-51, for a list of Old Testament scholars who concur. See also Currid, *Exodus*, 81 (quoting Calvin); Durham, 30-31; Andrew Bowling, *TWOT*, 465; Lewis Sperry Chafer, *Systematic Theology*, Vol. 3-4 (Grand Rapids: Kregel, 1976), 14, 21; Vol. 5-6, 30-33, liberally quoting with approval John Walvoord (*Outline of Christology*, unpublished ms., 6-8). Walvoord, in "Series in Christology – Part 4: The Preincarnate Son of God" (n. 5 at walvoord.com/article/31) lists numerous early church fathers who interpreted the OT theophanies, including the Angel in the burning bush, as the preincarnate Christ, e.g., Justin, Irenaeus, Tertullian, Clement of Alexandria,

messengers,[13] which proves that it denotes function more than form. Just as human envoys are not to be confused with the angelic species, neither is this matchless Messenger of Yahweh.

Exodus 3 does not present the Angel of Yahweh as a created being, relaying the words of a God who remains in heaven. Verse 2 indeed introduces Him, "And the Angel of Yahweh appeared to him in a flame of fire out of the midst of the bush...." But in verse 4, "*God* called to him out of the bush." In verse 5, the ground is holy because the holy God is present. And in verse 6, Moses is afraid to look, not at a created angel: "And Moses hid his face, because he was afraid to look at *God*." God was in there. From the bush, verse 7, "Then *Yahweh* said...." The Angel of Yahweh is God. The Messenger of Yahweh is the I AM who I AM.

Remember, Yahweh is a holy Trinity. The peculiar honor which the Father bestowed upon His Son is for Him to be the One who images forth His glory. That did not begin at Christmas. It did not begin, period. It has always been true. God the Son, *the Word*, has always been both the Messenger and the Message. We see the Trinitarian relationship also in Zechariah 1:12-13:

> Then the Angel of Yahweh said, 'O Yahweh of hosts, how long will you have no mercy on Jerusalem and the cities of Judah, against which you have been angry these seventy years?' [13]And Yahweh answered gracious and comforting words to the Angel who talked with me.

There the Angel of Yahweh is a distinct Person, interceding for His people, praying to Yahweh the Father and receiving an answer (for the sake of His audience, like John 11:41-42). Thus Zechariah

---

and the synod of Antioch. Juncker adds Athanasius and Eusebius (244, see also my n. 3, above), saying "the title Angel reveals an extremely early and widely accepted Christology" (227).

12. See Andrew Bowling, *TWOT*, 464-465; Hans Bietenhard, *NIDNTT*, 1:101-103.

13. In the OT, about half the uses of *mal'ak* are of human messengers, e.g., Num. 20:14, 22:5, Judg. 7:24; 1 Sam. 6:21; 1 Ki. 19:2. For the Greek *angelos* as humans, see Mt. 11:10, Mk. 1:2, Lk. 7:24, 27; 9:52; Jas. 2:25.

shows Yahweh in relationship with Yahweh, just as our Trinitarian faith expects (cf. Jn. 1:1, "and the Word was *with* God").

We maintain orthodoxy by again emphasizing that the title "Angel" does not denote essence as a type of *created* being. It denotes the function of a messenger. God the Son is the Angel of Yahweh, *uncreated* and self-sufficient, eternally related to the Father, equal in essence and obedient in role. The Father sends, and the Son goes out as a Messenger to reveal the Godhead.[14]

To Hagar. After Abram allowed Sarai to mistreat her misused maidservant, Hagar fled from her (Gen. 16:6). "The Angel of Yahweh found her" (16:7) and commanded her to return to Sarai submissively (16:9). "The Angel of Yahweh also said to her, "I will surely multiply your seed..." (16:10). How could a created angel do that? Does not Yahweh alone create life? The Angel did not say, "Thus says the LORD." He said, "I will multiply," because He is Yahweh Himself. The Scripture clarifies, "So she called the Name of *Yahweh who spoke to her El Ro'i* [God of Seeing], for she said, 'Have I really here seen Him who sees me?'" (16:13, AT).[15] John Currid explains her question is "awkward Hebrew and, thus, difficult to translate. Even so, its meaning is clear: Hagar is surprised that she has survived her encounter *with Yahweh.*"[16] When the Angel of Yahweh appeared to Hagar, she saw the all-seeing *God* (cf. Jn. 1:48, Rev. 5:6).

At the near sacrifice of Isaac, "the Angel of Yahweh called to [Abraham] from heaven," stopped him, and commended him because: "you have not withheld your son, your only son, from

---

14. Hence Jesus' frequent title for the Father, "the One who sent Me" (e.g., Jn. 4:34, 7:16, 29).

15. Cf. ESV footnote for this alternative, literal translation of the Hebrew.

16. *Genesis*, 307 (emphasis mine). Earlier, Currid commented: "This is the first appearance of that being in Scripture. This Angel is identified with God later in the passage (16:13), and he speaks as if he is God (16:10-12). That identification is made elsewhere in the Bible (see Exod. 3:2; Judg. 13:17-22). To put it simply, the Angel of Yahweh is a manifestation of Yahweh himself.... A strong argument can be made that the Angel of Yahweh is the Second Person of the Trinity, a pre-incarnate Christ. As John Calvin

me" (Gen. 22:11-12). By not withholding Isaac from *God* (cf. 22:1), he was not withholding Isaac from the Angel of Yahweh, because the Angel of Yahweh is God the Son.

To Jacob. When Jacob stole Esau's firstborn blessing and fled from his revenge, Yahweh appeared to Jacob at a place he renamed *Bethel*, which means "House of God" (Gen. 28:10-19). Then, when Jacob's father-in-law Laban was cheating him, "the Angel of God" spoke to him in a dream and said, "I am the God of Bethel" (31:11-13). The Angel identified Himself as Yahweh, the God who appeared to Jacob at Bethel.

When Jacob fled from Laban and feared Esau's approaching camp, he prayed to Yahweh in humility for deliverance (32:9-12). "That same night... Jacob was left alone. And a man wrestled with him until the break of the day" (32:22, 24). At the end of the struggle, the "Man" renamed Jacob "Isra*el*," which means, "He strives with *God*." The "Man" explained, "for you have striven with *God*..." (v. 28). "So Jacob called the name of the place *Peniel* ['the face of God'], saying, 'For *I have seen God* face to face, and yet my life has been delivered!'" (v. 30). The "Man" was identified as God in the same manner that One of the three "men" who appeared to Abraham in Genesis 18 was actually Yahweh. Just as Hagar was surprised to have survived an encounter with God, so was Jacob, who knew he had not wrestled with a mortal man, but with God Himself, the pre-incarnate Son. Hosea 12:3-4 recounts this episode with a telling parallelism: "... he strove with God. He strove with the Angel...." The "Man" was "the Angel," who is "God." After mentioning the Angel, Hosea continued, "He met Him[17] [the Angel] at Bethel, and there God spoke with us – Yahweh, the God of hosts, Yahweh is his memorial name" (12:4-5). The "Man" is "the Angel" is "God" is "Yahweh."

---

remarks... 'The ancient teachers of the Church have rightly understood [it to be] the Eternal Son of God in respect to his office as Mediator'" (304-305).

17. ESV translates, "He met God," but footnotes the literal Hebrew, "He met *him*." Their mistranslation confuses the antecedent: the Angel is the One most recently mentioned.

These encounters with Yahweh, manifested in His Messenger, so impacted Jacob that, at the end of his life, while prophetically blessing his grandsons (Gen. 48:15-16), he invoked another insightful parallelism:

> "The *God* before whom my fathers Abraham and Isaac walked,
> the *God* who has been my shepherd all my life...
> [16]the *Angel* who has redeemed me from all evil, bless the boys....

Jacob again equated the Angel with God. The Angel was able to "bless" Joseph's boys because He is their covenant God. The Angel "redeemed" Jacob from all evil as a foreshadow of the Angel's redemption of Israel in the Exodus.

At the Exodus. We have already seen that the Angel of Yahweh is the Yahweh who appeared to Moses and identified Himself as the I AM (Ex. 3:2-15). In the actual exodus, "Yahweh brought the people of Israel out of the land of Egypt" (Ex. 12:51) in the Person of "the Messenger of God, who was going before the army of Israel" (14:19, AT).[18] The Angel was the One manifesting in the glory cloud and pillar of fire (cf. 14:19, 24). After the giving of the Law, Yahweh said:

> "Behold, I send an angel before you to guard you on the way and to bring you to the place that I have prepared. [21]Pay careful attention to him and obey his voice; do not rebel against him, for he will not pardon your transgression, for my name is in him" (23:20-21).

To rebel against this Angel is to rebel against Yahweh, because Yahweh's Name is in the Angel, which means "he possesses the full, revealed divine nature," and, "He is to be reverentially accorded full divine honours."[19] Thus, prominent Old Testament scholar Gerhard von Rad taught that Yahweh and His Angel are "obviously one and the same."[20] John Durham concludes that saying Yahweh's

---

18. Currid (*Exodus*, 300), Motyer (*Exodus*, 51), and the *ESV Study Bible* (167) all connect the Angel in Ex. 14:19 with 3:2.

19. Motyer, *The Message of Exodus*, 246 and 51 (respectively).

Name is within the Angel "is virtually an assertion of equivalence: the 'messenger' = Yahweh."[21]

We can rejoice in another layer of fulfillment: the Angel of Yahweh became flesh, a God-Man named *Yeshua*, and the Name *Yahweh* is literally "in" *Yeshua* ("Yahweh saves"), just as the fullness of His Being dwells in Him.[22] *Jude 5 (ESV)[23] confirms that Jesus is the Angel of Yahweh, who is Yahweh, who led the people out of Egypt:*

> Now I want to remind you, although you once fully knew it, that *Jesus, who saved a people out of the land of Egypt,* afterward destroyed those who did not believe.

Jude was one of Jesus' "brothers," who did not believe in Jesus at first (Jn. 7:5). But after Jesus' resurrection, he came to understand that Jesus is more than his human brother; Jesus is the eternal God who delivered His people through the Exodus and later punished that generation's unbelief!

Paul taught the same thing as Jude in 1 Corinthians 10. The Israelite forefathers passed through the Red Sea under the glory

---

20. *TDNT* 1:77-78, qtd. in Durham, 335.

21. *Ibid.*, 335. Motyer footnotes: "Note how in 23:20-26 the angel and the Lord alternate– his presence, my name, his voice, I speak, etc. According to Cassuto, 'In the final analysis, the angel… is simply God's action.' Mackay, surely correctly, sees the Angel as 'a temporary, pre-incarnate, appearance of the second person of the Trinity'" (*The Message of Exodus*, 245).

22. Mt. 1:21 (treated on p. 60; cf. K. H. Rengstorf, *NIDNTT*, 2:330-332, who says, "It is the oldest name containing the divine name Yahweh… cf. the vb. *yāša'*, help, save" [331]). Cf. also Lk. 1:31, 2:11; 1 Tim. 1:15; Col. 2:9, 1:19.

23. Some ancient manuscripts have *Kurios* ("Lord") instead of *Iēsous* ("Jesus"), and so some translations render "Lord" instead of "Jesus" (e.g., NASB, HCSB). Gathercole (*The Preexistent Son*, 40) notes that the immediately preceding verse ended with "our only Master and Lord, Jesus Christ" (Jude 4), so even if the original was *Kurios*, Jude would still be talking about Jesus! In a three-two split, the UBS Editorial Committee chose *Kurios* for USB⁴, NA²⁷. But Bruce Metzger wrote in the minority report, "Critical principles seem to require the adoption of Ἰησοῦς, which admittedly is the best attested reading among Greek and versional witnesses" (*A Textual Commentary on the Greek New Testament*, Second Edition [Stuttgart: German Bible Society, 1994], 657). It also makes more sense that a scribe would change *Iēsous* to *Kurios* than the other way around. Therefore, ESV, NET, and NLT sided with the Committee's minority and rendered "Jesus." See Gathercole (36-40) for a thorough summary of the overwhelming

cloud, "and all drank the same spiritual drink. For they drank from the spiritual Rock that followed them, and *the Rock was Christ*" (v. 4). Because Yahweh stood on the rock that dispensed living water to save the Israelites in the wilderness (Ex. 17:6), Yahweh later became known as "the Rock" (Deut. 32:4, 15, 18, 30-31). So Paul is doing something bigger than typology here. Surely Paul did not think a physical rock "followed" the people; the "Rock" was a Person, so named by Moses. Therefore, Paul taught that Jesus Christ is the Yahweh of Exodus 17, Numbers 20, and Deuteronomy 32. This becomes even clearer a few verses later: "We must not put Christ to the test, *as some of them did* and were destroyed by serpents, nor grumble, as some of them did and were destroyed by the Destroyer" (1 Cor. 10:9).[24] Again, Christ is the Yahweh of the Exodus generation!

To Balaam. When Israel was in the wilderness, they defeated the Amorites because the sovereign I AM had given them into their hands (Num. 21:34). The Moabites and Midianites were so scared that they hired the pagan prophet Balaam, "who loved gain from wrongdoing" (2 Pet. 2:15), to curse the Israelites (Num. 22:1-7).

> But God's anger was kindled because he went, and the Angel of Yahweh took his stand in the way as his adversary. Now he was riding on the donkey, and his two servants were with him. [23]And the donkey saw the Angel of Yahweh standing in the road, with a drawn sword in his hand.... [31]Then Yahweh opened the eyes of Balaam, and he saw the Angel of Yahweh standing in the way, with his drawn sword in his hand. And he bowed down and fell on his face (Num. 22:22-23, 31).

The Angel of Yahweh rebuked Balaam and warned him to prophesy only the words *He* would give to bless and not curse

---

reasons to prefer "Jesus" as the original reading, where he cites Metzger and the two largest studies of the issue for support. See also the NET Bible study note and the *ESV Study Bible*. In 2012, the UBS Editorial Committee overturned its previous decision and placed *Iēsous* in NA[28].

24. For textual criticism issues similar to Jude 5, see the impressive note in NET and also Gathercole, *The Preexistent Son*, 30.

Israel (22:32-35). Then, when words were given to Balaam, they came from Yahweh (23:5), because the Angel of Yahweh is Yahweh. This became even clearer when the same sword-wielding Angel appeared to Joshua.

To Joshua. Moses had prophesied, "Yahweh your God will raise up for you a prophet like me..." (Deut. 18:15-19). Before the death of Moses, Yahweh appointed Joshua to be that successor.[25] He promised Joshua, "Just as I was with Moses, so I will be with you" (Josh. 1:5). When it was time to cross the Jordan River and conquer Jericho, their first campaign into the Promised Land, "Yahweh said to Joshua, 'Today I will begin to exalt you in the sight of all Israel, that they may know that, as I was with Moses, so I will be with you'" (3:7). Then Yahweh performed another water miracle, splitting the Jordan River, and through Joshua's leadership, Israel crossed it on dry ground, just as they had at the Red Sea (chs. 3-4, esp. 4:14). And just as Moses met Yahweh in the Person of the Angel of Yahweh in the burning bush, so too did Joshua:

> When Joshua was by Jericho, he lifted up his eyes and looked, and behold, a Man was standing before him with His drawn sword in His hand. And Joshua went to Him and said to Him, "Are you for us, or for our adversaries?" [14]And He said, "No; but I am the Commander of the army of Yahweh. Now I have come." And Joshua fell on his face to the earth and worshiped and said to Him, "What does my Lord say to His servant?" [15]And the Commander of Yahweh's army said to Joshua, "Take off your sandals from your feet, because the place where you are standing is holy." And Joshua did so (5:13-15, AT).

This "Man" was the same Angel of Yahweh with His sword drawn as appeared to Balaam. This Commander of Yahweh's

---

25. Num. 27:15-23, Deut. 1:38, 3:28, 31:1-8, 34:9. Interestingly, Joshua's original name was *Hoshea* ("He saves," Num. 13:8), but Moses renamed him *Yehoshua* ("Yahweh saves," 13:16), a variant of the same Hebrew name for Jesus! In the Greek NT both are represented by the same *Iēsous* (cf. Acts 7:45). Joshua was a foreshadow of Jesus, the ultimate Prophet "like Moses," but greater, performing a greater Exodus and securing the Promised Land of New Jerusalem (cf. Jn. 6:14, 7:40; Acts 3:20-26, 7:37, esp. 7:39).

angelic army was no mere man, nor mere created angel, and Joshua realized that, so he *worshiped* Him. Joshua knew only the One true God is worthy of worship, and he knew this was God. A regular, created angel would have stopped Joshua from idolatrous worship (cf. Rev. 19:10, 22:8-9). But this Angel did not stop Him, because it was not idolatry. It was appropriate to worship Him. He deserved it. He must be God!

Indeed, He commanded Joshua to take off his sandals because the ground was made holy by His presence, just as the Angel of Yahweh said to Moses in the burning bush (cf. Josh. 5:15, Ex. 3:5). Here was the promised Angel of Yahweh, in whom is Yahweh's Name, ready to lead His angelic army and His people to victory, fulfilling His covenant with Abraham to grace them with the land. Here was God the Son, pre-incarnate.

In Judges. After Joshua's generation and the unfaithful attempt to take the entire Promised Land, the Angel of Yahweh appeared in Judges 2:1-4 and introduced Himself, "I brought you up from Egypt and brought you into the land that I swore to give to your fathers" (v. 1). The Angel was the Yahweh who promised and delivered (cf. Ex. 20:2, Lev. 26:13). There He rebuked them for their faithlessness, and they wept.

Later, "the Angel of Yahweh came and sat under the terebinth" and "appeared" to Gideon (Judg. 6:11-12). After Gideon's reply, the title "the Angel of Yahweh" is replaced with, "And *Yahweh* turned to him and said…" (v. 14, also 16). In verse 20, He is "the Angel of God," and in vv. 21-22, "the Angel of Yahweh." The Angel turned Gideon's present to Him into a burnt offering to Yahweh and disappeared (6:21). Then Gideon exclaimed his fear and comfort from this face-to-face encounter (6:22-24).

Later still, the Angel of Yahweh appeared to Manoah and his barren wife in the form of "a Man" to announce the conception of Samson, who would be a Nazarite, consecrated to God (Judg.

13:2-20). Manoah offered to prepare Him a meal, not knowing who He was. The Angel said He would not eat it, and it would be more fitting to offer it as a burnt offering to Yahweh (13:15-16). When Manoah asked, "What is your name?" the Angel responded in a manner similar to His answer to the wrestling Jacob: "Why do you ask My Name, seeing it is wonderful?" (13:18).

We could possibly interpret this to mean that His Name was beyond comprehension, but the Name above all names is Yahweh, yet He enabled us to understand *it* (at least in glorious part). I think the Angel was helping to clue in Manoah, answering, in effect, "Why would you seek any name for Me other than the wonderful Name of Yahweh?" However slowly, Manoah and his wife arrived at this very revelation of the Messenger's identity. The Angel went up to heaven in the flame of the offering, and "they fell on their faces to the ground" (13:20).

> …Then Manoah knew that He was the Angel of Yahweh. [22]And Manoah said to his wife, "We shall surely die, for we have seen *God*." [23]But his wife said to him, "If *Yahweh* had meant to kill us, *He* would not have accepted a burnt offering and a grain offering at our hands, or shown us all these things, or now announced to us such things as these" (13:21-23).

They realized the Angel of Yahweh is Yahweh, who mercifully did not kill them, but announced gracious news of a deliverer's birth.

In the fiery furnace. In defiance of God's prophetic dream in chapter two, Nebuchadnezzar built a ninety-foot statue, entirely of gold (Dn. 3:1-7), representing him (cf. 2:37-38). He decreed that everyone in Babylon must fall down and worship the image. The Babylonian officials brought charges against Shadrach, Meshach, and Abednego for refusing to worship the idol (3:8-12). Threatened with death in a fiery furnace, they testified that their God was able to deliver them from it; but even if He did not, they would remain faithful (3:16-18). Nebuchadnezzar, filled with fury, ordered the furnace heated seven times hotter than usual, so much so that the soldiers who threw them into the furnace were themselves incinerated (3:19-22).

What happened next astonished the king: "I see four men unbound, walking in the midst of the fire, and they are not hurt; and the appearance of the fourth is like a son of the gods" (3:25). Later, he said their God "sent his angel and delivered" them (3:28). The report comes only from the lips of a pagan king (not yet humbled and restored, as in ch. 4); "for him the phrase 'like a son of the gods' is equivalent to 'like a divine being.'"[26] Was the fourth a created angel or the Angel of Yahweh? We cannot know with certainty, but I lean toward the uncreated Angel of Yahweh because of God's promise in Isaiah 43:2-3:

> When you pass through the waters, *I will be with you*;
>   and through the rivers, they shall not overwhelm you;
> *when you walk through fire* you shall not be burned,
>   and the flame shall not consume you.
> [3]*For I am Yahweh your God*,
>   the Holy One of Israel, your *Savior*.

Yahweh had promised to be with them in the fire, and I believe He was, in the Second Person of the Trinity, the Angel of Yahweh. He miraculously sustained His three servants, so they were not consumed like the pagan soldiers. Instead, they enjoyed a walk with their God – one has to wonder if the three Jews were sad to have to get out of the fiery furnace! The next appearance of Yahweh's Messenger in the book of Daniel lends credence to this possible interpretation of 3:25.

To Daniel. Two years into the rebuilding of the temple, after the return from exile, opposition led to a break in the work (Ezra 4:1-4, 24). This timing aligns with Daniel 10:1 and may be the cause of Daniel's twenty-one days of fasting and mourning (10:2-3).[27] Then:

[5]I lifted up my eyes and looked, and behold, a man clothed in linen, with a belt of fine gold from Uphaz around his waist. [6]His body was like beryl, his face like the appearance of lightning, his eyes like flaming torches, his arms and legs like the gleam of burnished bronze, and the sound of his words like the sound of a multitude.... [8]So I was left alone and saw this great vision, and no strength was left in me. My radiant appearance was fearfully changed [lit., my glory was changed to ruin], and I retained no strength. [9]...as I heard the sound of his words, I fell on my face in deep sleep with my face to the ground.

[10]And behold, a hand touched me and set me trembling on my hands and knees. [11]And he said to me, "O Daniel, man greatly loved, understand the words that I speak to you, and stand upright, for now I have been sent to you.... Fear not, Daniel, for from the first day that you set your heart to understand and humbled yourself before your God, your words have been heard, and I have come because of your words. [13]The prince of the kingdom of Persia withstood me twenty-one days, but Michael, one of the chief princes, came to help me, for I was left there with the kings of Persia, [14]and came to make you understand what is to happen to your people in the latter days. For the vision is for days yet to come."

[15]When he had spoken to me according to these words, I turned my face toward the ground and was mute. [16]And behold, one in the likeness of the [sons] of man touched my lips. Then I opened my mouth and spoke. I said to him who stood before me, "O my lord, by reason of the vision pains have come upon me, and I retain no strength. [17]How can my lord's servant talk with my lord? For now no strength remains in me, and no breath is left in me."

[18]Again one having the appearance of a man touched me and strengthened me. [19]And he said, "O man greatly loved, fear not, peace be with you; be strong and of good courage." And

---

26. NET Bible study note on Dan. 3:25.

27. This section borrows from the author's Sunday School teaching, "Daniel 10: God-given Revelation of the Heavenly/Earthly War," 2 Sept 2012 (ProjectOne28.com/dan10).

as he spoke to me, I was strengthened and said, "Let my lord speak, for you have strengthened me." [20]Then he said, "Do you know why I have come to you? But now I will return to fight against the prince of Persia; and when I go out, behold, the prince of Greece will come. [21]But I will tell you what is inscribed in the book of truth: there is none who contends by my side against these except Michael, your prince.

Who is this? Is this figure created or divine? Ronald Wallace sets up the interpretive tension:

> The exact identity of this figure is left vague. He uses the same manner of approach, the same kind of words, and exercises the... same ministry as the angel Gabriel. Yet, throughout the Bible, it is the presence of God alone which produces such humbling and shattering experience, and it is God alone who can comfort and strengthen in such a way. The prophets had this kind of experience when they were in the presence of God himself.[28]

But 10:13 says a demonic angel "withstood me twenty-one days," so Michael helped. Therefore, the *ESV Study Bible* concludes:

> Yet this glorious figure was unable to complete his task without the help of Michael, one of the chief princes (v. 13), so it is unlikely that this is a physical manifestation of God or Christ. More probably, he is one of the angelic attendants of God, who reflect their master's glory.

On which side should we land? The decisive, Scriptural consideration comes in Revelation 1:12-17. John reports his heavenly vision of the resurrected, glorified Jesus Christ with virtually the exact language as Daniel 10, causing even the same response, as the accompanying table shows.[29]

---

28. Ronald Wallace, *The Message of Daniel* (Downers Grove: IVP, 1984), 173 (Is. 6:4-8; Je. 1:6-10; Ezk. 2:1, 2).

29. See also the chart comparing these descriptions in Daniel 10 and Revelation 1 with the vision of God in Ezekiel 1 in Andrew E. Steinmann, *Daniel* (St. Louis, MO: Concordia Publishing House, 2008), 499.

DANIEL		REVELATION	
10:5	clothed in linen	1:13	clothed in a long robe
10:5	belt of gold around waist	1:13	belt of gold around chest
10:6	eyes like flaming torches	1:14	eyes like a flame of fire
7:9	hair white like wool	1:14	hairs white like wool, like snow
10:6	face like lightning	1:16	face shining like the sun
10:6	arms/legs like burnished bronze	1:15	feet like burnished bronze
10:6	voice like the sound... multitude	1:15	voice like the sound... waters
10:9	I fell on my face in a deep sleep	1:17	I fell at His feet like a dead man
10:10	a hand touched me	1:17	He placed His hand on me
10:12	"Do not fear..."	1:17	"Do not fear..."

Because of Revelation 1, there should be no doubt that the "Man clothed in linen" in Daniel 10 is the pre-incarnate Christ.[30] Many agree, and the ones who disagree on the grounds that He was "withstood" do not need to let that override Revelation 1. First, we have already seen the Messenger of Yahweh introduce Himself as the Commander of Yahweh's army with a weapon in His hand (Josh. 5:13-14). What is supernatural battle like? What is His role in it? I have no idea, but the imagery portrays the pre-incarnate Son ready "to fight," as in Daniel 10:20.

Secondly, it is not impossible or illogical that the Son of God was being withstood. Is this really any different than what we know has been going on since Satan first rebelled? Why did God not immediately annihilate the demons? Why does He continue to sustain them with power to resist? Why does He restrain His

---

30. See also the case in Steinmann (497-501), who cites also Miller and Young. *Pace* James M. Hamilton, Jr., *With the Clouds of Heaven: The Book of Daniel in Biblical Theology*, New Studies in Biblical Theology, ed. D. A. Carson (Downers Grove, IL: InterVarsity Press, 2014), 144-46. Hamilton's reason for disbelief is that Daniel does not explicitly link the figure in 10:5-6 with 7:13-14 (as he connected Gabriel in 9:21

infinite power, which could prevent the demons from doing anything bad? Why does He so often let the leash out a little bit, so that the enemy can steal and kill and harm like it did with Job? I personally do not see a new problem with the interpretation that the Son of God was being busied for twenty-one days in the angelic war. It is a very vivid presentation of the mystery, but not a new mystery.

Furthermore, the problem shifts little if we say some amazingly glorious, god-like angel was delayed – why did God not give that angel the power to overcome the prince of Persia immediately, so that he was not delayed? If God did not want a twenty-one-day delay, then there would not have been a twenty-one-day delay, because the all-powerful God rules over all He has created, even demons. So with due respect to the *ESV Study Bible*, we need not believe this passage means this Being was "unable" to win on His own. What we do need to believe is the clarity of Revelation 1: Daniel saw the pre-incarnate Son of God, who later became the God-Man, died for sins, was raised again, and was seen by John. Someday soon, we will see Him, too!

"THE ANGEL OF YAHWEH" AS YAHWEH	
GENESIS 16:7-13	NUMBERS 22:22-31
18:1-33	JOSHUA 5:13-15
22:1-12	JUDGES 2:1-4
31:11-13	6:11-24
32:22-30	13:2-23
48:15-16	DANIEL 3:25-28
EXODUS 3:1-15	10:5-21
14:19-24	HOSEA 12:3-5
23:20-21	

In the New Testament. We have seen that the Angel of Yahweh was a major character in the Old Testament. Yet He is never delineated as such in the New Testament.[31] What happened? Did

---

with 8:16), an argument from silence on, it seems to me, an artificial requirement. He concludes that this Daniel 10 figure is a created angel who reflects the Son's glory (seen in Rev. 1) like the angel in Revelation 10 reflects it. But see G. K. Beale's compelling case that the "angel" in Revelation 10 *is* the divine Son of Man in Revelation 1 and Daniel 10 (*The Book of Revelation*, NIGCT [Grand Rapids, MI: Eerdmans, 1999], 522-525).

He retire? No, He was even more present and active than ever – in the Person of Jesus Christ! Motyer sums up the correlation well:

> …We can put it this way: the Angel suffers no reduction or adjustment of his full deity, yet he is that mode of deity whereby the holy God can keep company with sinners.
>
> There is only one other in the Bible who is both identical with and yet distinct from the Lord. One who, without abandoning the full essence and prerogatives of deity or diminishing the divine holiness, is able to accommodate himself to the company of sinners and who, while affirming the wrath of God, is yet a supreme display of his outreaching mercy. Such indeed is the Angel of the Lord as revealed in the Old Testament, and, consequently, Barton Payne rightly does not hesitate to say these 'revelations of the unique Angel… can be appreciated only when understood as a pre-incarnate appearance of Jesus Christ.'[32]

---

31. Cf. Walvoord, qtd. in Chafer, *op. cit.*, Vol. 5-6, 32. Against Michael Bird, who says, "*The* angel of the Lord is active in predicting Jesus' birth and resurrection in such a way that it was unlikely that confusion of the two ever entered the Evangelists' minds (see Matt 1:20, 23 [*sic*, 24]; 2:13, 19; 28:2; Luke 1:11; 2:9)" ("Of God, Angels, and Men," *How God Became Jesus: The Real Origins of Belief in Jesus' Divine Nature – A Response to Bart Ehrman*, ed. Michael F. Bird [Grand Rapids, MI: Zondervan, 2014], 37, emphasis mine). In truth, the Greek definite article is not present in Mt. 1:20 (or 2:13, 19; 28:2; Lk. 1:11), so all major translations render, "*an* angel of the Lord," not to be identified with "the Angel of Yahweh" in the OT. The Greek article in 1:24 is anaphoric, pointing back to the created angel of 1:20 (see Daniel B. Wallace, *Greek Grammar Beyond the Basics: An Exegetical Syntax of the New Testament* [Grand Rapids, MI: Zondervan, 1996], 217-218). *Pace* Wallace, 252, where he argues that the LXX translated "the Angel of the Lord" without the article, as in Mt. 1:20. If one agrees exegetically, as Wallace does (252, n. 97), that the Angel of Yahweh is Yahweh Himself, then He is the Son, not the one announcing the Son's birth. The linguistic argument of Wallace, *et al.*, is impossible theologically and unnecessary grammatically. I maintain with the many: *the* Angel of Yahweh is not present in the NT, except in the Person of the Son of God, Jesus Christ. Michael Bird's overall treatment of "the Angel of the Lord" is poor; e.g., "Paradoxically the angel of the Lord both *is* YHWH and *is not* YHWH" (37, emphasis his). That is uncareful, untrue, and inferior to, "The Angel of YHWH *is* YHWH *in relationship with* YHWH (cf. Jn. 1:1)."

32. Motyer, *Exodus*, 51, citing J. B. Payne, *The Theology of the Old Testament* (Zondervan, 1962), 170. Conscientious students may gasp at the use of the word "mode," but I assure you that Dr. Motyer is an orthodox Trinitarian, not a modalist. Also, the "only one other who is both identical with and yet distinct from the Lord" is not technically correct, given that the Holy Spirit is also identical and distinct. But the Spirit is not the One who images forth the Trinity as the Son does, so the thrust of the quote from Motyer is true.

Prophecies of the Messiah as God-Man

As unfathomable as it may have been, numerous places in the Old Testament prophesied that God Himself would become the Messiah, the ultimate prophetic, priestly King of Israel who would atone for His people's sins and conquer their enemies.

Psalm 45. According to its superscription, Psalm 45 was composed as a love song for the Son of David, the Messianic King of Israel, and His bride. After extolling the King as most handsome, gracious, and victorious, it escalates surprisingly in verses 6-8:

> Your throne, O God, is forever and ever.
>> The scepter of your kingdom is a scepter of uprightness;
>> [7]you have loved righteousness and hated wickedness.
> Therefore God, your God, has anointed you
>> with the oil of gladness beyond your companions;
>> [8]your robes are all fragrant with myrrh and aloes and cassia.
> From ivory palaces stringed instruments make you glad....

The Davidic King is addressed as God (v. 6) in relationship with God (v. 7; cf. Jn. 1:1). Is the psalmist exaggerating about a mere human? Would such blasphemy be tolerated in the Hebrew canonical Scriptures? Raymond C. Ortlund, Jr., dismisses the thought:

> The eternality of his sovereign reign is the point of the verse, consistent with the grandeur of the psalm as a whole, and the historic sons of David were not deified. The uniqueness of Israel's God was too clear to allow confusion on the matter, and the weaknesses of Israel's Kings were too obvious for ancient Near Eastern ideological bluff.[33]

The natural meaning is that God would become a God-Man, a descendent of David who reigns forever in righteous, sovereign gladness! The Spirit-inspired writer of Hebrews 1:8-9 quoted this passage and applied it to Jesus, who is infinitely superior to the

---

33. "The Deity of Christ and the Old Testament," in *The Deity of Christ*, 46.

angels because He is God the Son, the radiance of God's glory and the exact representation of His being (1:3; see pp. 138-139).

Isaiah 7. In c. 735 B.C., Ahaz, king of Judah, feared the northern alliance of Syria and Israel (the ten northern tribes in the divided kingdom). They were trying to force Judah into their alliance against the growing super-power, Assyria. The prophet Isaiah ministered in this context, calling Ahaz not to fear these nations, which would pass away under the Lord's judgment, but instead, to stand firm in faith (7:1-9).

> Again Yahweh spoke to Ahaz, [11]"Ask a sign of Yahweh your God; let it be deep as Sheol or high as heaven." [12]But Ahaz said, "I will not ask, and I will not put Yahweh to the test" (7:10-12).

Yahweh was prepared to demonstrate His commitment with a sign as big as Ahaz could imagine, but Ahaz piously pretended the request would be sinful. In truth, Ahaz was disobeying Yahweh's command, "Ask," because he did not want a sign; he did not want to believe. He wanted to trust Assyria for protection from Israel/Syria instead of trusting Yahweh. Therefore, Isaiah prophesied against him that Yahweh would whistle for Assyria to come against Israel, Syria, and Judah (7:16-25). In unbelief, Ahaz refused the offer of a positive sign, so Yahweh promised him a negative sign instead in 7:13-14:

> And he said, "Hear then, O house of David! Is it too little for you to weary men, that you weary my God also? [14]Therefore the Lord himself will give you a sign. Behold, the virgin shall conceive and bear a son, and shall call his name Immanuel."

Before this miraculous child grew up, the Davidic throne would lose its sovereignty, becoming a puppet to Assyria (7:16–8:8). When this child came of age, the people of Judah would be able to look back at the Assyrian conquests and know that Yahweh brought about those events in judgment against them.

Some have argued that the Hebrew behind "virgin" implies nothing more than a young woman of marriageable age. They assume the woman would conceive in the natural manner of sexual relations with a man. They find its fulfillment in the next chapter, in which Isaiah went into his wife and conceived another son with similar sign value (8:3-4). First, we must wonder what kind of a "sign" it would be from Yahweh that a non-virgin, married woman conceived in the same manner as millions before and after her. Not exactly the "deep as Sheol or high as heaven" kind of sign that was first offered (7:11). Secondly, Motyer has demonstrated that the Hebrew word "*'almâ* is not a general term meaning 'young woman' but a specific one meaning 'virgin.' It is worth noting that outside the Bible, 'so far as may be ascertained,' *'almâ* was 'never used of a married woman.'"[34] We ought not consider Isaiah's son to be the fulfillment of 7:14. That child's mother was not a virgin, nor was he the King connected to this prophecy in 8:8-10[35] and 9:6.

Immanuel means "God with us." Was that metaphorical? Would God simply be present with His people through the work of the human king, or would the Child be God incarnate? He is addressed in 8:8 as the owner of the land of Judah and in 8:10 as the reason why their enemies will fail. Whereas this could be spoken of a human king, the definitive reason to believe He is a God-Man is that "it is impossible to separate this Immanuel from the Davidic king whose birth delivers his people... and whose complex name includes the designation Mighty God" in 9:6.[36] Therefore, Matthew (1:20-23) accurately reported the angel's explanation:

> "Joseph, son of David, do not fear to take Mary as your wife, for that which is conceived in her is from the Holy Spirit...."
> [22]All this took place to fulfill what the Lord had spoken by the prophet:

34. Motyer, *Isaiah*, 85, see esp. his treatment of the various Hebrew words in Gen. 24:14-43. Cf. Alexander A. MacRae, *TWOT*, 672.

35. Ortlund, after mentioning that Isaiah's wife was not a virgin, adds, "It also seems odd

> [23]"Behold, the virgin shall conceive and bear a son,
>   and they shall call his name Immanuel"

(which means, God with us).

More than 700 years in advance, Isaiah prophesied that God would become a Man in the womb of a virgin: Jesus Christ in the virgin Mary!

Isaiah 9. The prophetic promise of victory through this God-Child continued. Zebulun and Naphtali, the northernmost tribes of Israel, would be the first to be carried into exile by Assyria, who would resettle other captive foreigners into their land. That is why it came to be called "Galilee of the Gentiles" (Isa. 9:1). But Isaiah promised their land would also be the first to be made glorious with the light of salvation (9:1-2; this is why Jesus began His ministry there, Mt. 4:12-16). They would rejoice like victors dividing spoil (Isa. 9:3) "because" the yoke and burden of the oppressor has been broken (9:4, New Exodus language, cf. Lev. 26:13). Battle gear will be discarded in peace "because" of this virgin-child (9:6, AT):

> Because ,a, Child is born to us;
>   ,a, Son is given to us;
> and the government will be upon His shoulder,
>   and His Name will be called
> Wonderful Counselor, Warrior God,
>   Father ,of, Eternity, Prince ,of, Peace.

This description is so astounding that translators and interpreters have stumbled over it. Ortlund says the Septuagint "seems downright confused," the "Targum evades the import of the Hebrew," and the "Vulgate fails to discern the structure of the Hebrew."[37] Some Jewish teachers tried to translate "Warrior God" as "mighty hero" or "mighty chief" and apply the passage to King

---

that Isaiah's son would be addressed in royal terms: 'Your land, O Immanuel' (Isa. 8:8)' (*op cit.*, 56). Ortlund, however, leaves open the possibility that 7:14 was fulfilled in Isaiah's son and picked up typologically by Matthew. I favor instead Motyer's case that this prophecy was singularly fulfilled in Jesus (84-87, esp. because of Isa. 9:6-7).

36. Motyer, *Isaiah*, 86.

Hezekiah. But he "cannot be the king Isaiah is referring to, because the endless triumph of verse 7 goes far beyond the accomplishment of any historic son of David...."[38]

The Hebrew behind "Warrior God," *'el gibbôr*, was first ascribed to Yahweh in Deuteronomy 10:17.[39] The same title appears in Isaiah 10:21,[40] obviously applied to the Yahweh of 10:20. Therefore, the prophesy in 9:6 should be unmistakable: Yahweh will become a God-Man to defeat His people's enemies and establish unending, ever-increasing peace! Notice the "Child is born," but the eternal Son did not begin, so it shifts to the "Son is *given*" – "because in this manner God loved the world: that He *gave* His One-of-a-kind Son" (Jn. 3:16, lit.). In this God-Man, Yeshua Messiah, dwells the fullness of the Godhead: the Son, the "Wonderful Counselor" (Holy Spirit),[41] and the "Father of Eternity"[42] – Three in One.

Isaiah 35 and 40. Numerous passages promised that Yahweh would come to His people, visibly and victoriously.

> A voice cries:
> "In the wilderness prepare the way of Yahweh;
>> make straight in the desert a highway for our God.
> [4]Every valley shall be lifted up,
>> and every mountain and hill be made low;
> the uneven ground shall become level,
>> and the rough places a plain.

---

37. *Op. cit.*, 50. Juncker, *op. cit.*, "It may be that they [trans. of Vaticanus] balked at attributing Deity to Messiah, for the Hebrew is not exceptionally difficult and the title... ["Mighty God"] is translated correctly in 10:21" (225, n. 13).

38. Ortlund, 51.

39. So, Ortlund, 51, who adds, "In the usage of Isaiah, the word *'el* always refers to deity...." For *gibbôr* as "warrior," see Motyer, *Isaiah*, 102; Oswalt, *TWOT*, 148.

40. Motyer, *Isaiah*, 102.

41. When Jesus said the Father "will give you *another* Counselor" (Jn. 14:16, identified as the Holy Spirit, 14:26, 15:26, 16:7), He communicates that He (Jesus) is the Counselor of Isaiah 9:6, as is the Holy Spirit, who is distinct but united with Him in the Trinity.

42. Jn. 10:38, 14:10, 17:21, 22, 23; for "fullness," see Col. 2:9, 1:19.

> [5]And the glory of Yahweh shall be revealed,
>   and all flesh shall see it together,
>   for the mouth of Yahweh has spoken" (Isa. 40:3-5).

All four Gospels quote this passage to explain the forerunner ministry of John the Baptist. If John was the voice to prepare the way for Yahweh, and he introduced Jesus, then Jesus is Yahweh!

> [2]…They will see the glory of Yahweh,
>   the majesty of our God.
> [4]…Behold, your God
>   will come with vengeance,
> with the recompense of God.
>   He will come and save you.
> [5]Then the eyes of the blind shall be opened,
>   and the ears of the deaf unstopped;
> [6]then shall the lame man leap like a deer,
>   and the tongue of the mute sing for joy.
> For waters break forth in the wilderness,
>   and streams in the desert… (Isa. 35:2-6).

After performing these miracles, Jesus alluded to this prophecy to answer John the Baptist's request for verification, to prove that He was not only the Messiah, but Yahweh come to save![43]

Isaiah 53: The Arm of Yahweh. The rich history of this metaphor is requisite for understanding its ultimate fulfillment. In promising the Exodus, Yahweh said, "I will redeem you with an outstretched *arm*…" (Ex. 6:6). Moses reminded the second generation, "Yahweh your God brought you out from there with a mighty hand and an outstretched *arm*."[44] Yahweh is Spirit and does not literally have a flesh-and-bones arm, but it metaphorically stands for His great power at work in Creation (Jer. 27:5, 32:17) and salvation through judgment. In Jeremiah, the promised exile was a reverse Exodus: "I myself will fight against you with outstretched hand and strong arm, in anger and in fury and in great wrath"

---

43. Lk. 7:18-27, esp. vv. 21, 27

44. Dt. 5:15, cf. 7:19, 9:29, 11:2, 26:8; 1 Ki. 8:42, 17:36; 2 Chron. 6:32, Ps. 136:2

(21:5). After Isaiah prophesied the exile, he modeled the people's prayer, which parallels *arm* and *salvation*:

> O Yahweh, be gracious to us; we wait for you.
>> Be our arm every morning,
>> our salvation in the time of trouble (33:2).

The Gospel of Isaiah 40 is, "Behold, the Lord Yahweh comes with might, and His Arm rules for Him…" (v. 10). God's promise in 51:5 again connects arm and salvation through judgment:

> My righteousness draws near,
>> my salvation has gone out,
>> and my arms will judge the peoples;
> the coastlands hope for me,
>> and for my arm they wait.

Isaiah 51:9 prays for the New Exodus, "Awake, awake, put on strength, O Arm of Yahweh; awake, as in days of old…." The context continues in remembrance of the judgment and redemption of the original Exodus. For the vindication of His Name, the evangelists' "Behold your God!" in 40:9 is mirrored in Yahweh's "Behold Me!" (52:6, AT). The content of "the Gospel of happiness" is the reign of God (52:7) and "the return of Yahweh to Zion" (52:8) in the New Exodus (52:9-12).

> Yahweh bared His holy Arm
>> before the eyes of all the nations,
> and all the ends of the earth will see
>> the salvation of our God (52:10, AT).

The metaphor of Yahweh's Arm is woven into Biblical history from the Exodus throughout the book of Isaiah. What we must recognize is that the Arm of Yahweh is Yahweh Himself. No one could say of my arm, "That's not Spencer. That's just an arm." My arm is part of my person. Likewise, the Arm of Yahweh is Yahweh personally and powerfully at work.[45]

---

45. Cf. Motyer, *Isaiah*, 409, 427.

Isaiah 52 celebrates the Gospel, "Yahweh has bared His holy Arm." As the means of the New Exodus is unpacked, the "Behold Me" (52:6) shifts to, "Behold, My Servant" (52:13). The focus of our study comes in Isaiah 53:1, "Who has believed what he heard from us? And to whom has the Arm of Yahweh been revealed?" We must notice the following verse begins with an explanatory conjunction, "For," giving the reason why the Gospel message met with unbelief. *"For he [the Servant, the Arm, v. 1] grew up before him [Yahweh] like a young plant, and like a root out of dry ground" (53:2).* Motyer sums up the confusion that naturally results unless God opens our eyes:

> Why did the message of the Servant and the revelation of him as 'the Arm' meet with dismissiveness? First, he seemed to have a wholly earthly or natural origin; the imagery of growth out of the soil points to a human 'family tree' (cf. 'is not this the carpenter's son?', Mt. 13:55). How could a mere man be 'the Arm of the Lord'? Secondly, he grew up before him, i.e., before the Lord. How can he be 'the Arm of the Lord' if he is a distinct person over against the Lord, growing up in his presence?[46]

Thirdly, Motyer continues with the second half of 53:2, explaining that He had no physical beauty that attracted the people to Him. *But the reality remains that in the movement from Isaiah 52:6 through 53:2 the Arm of Yahweh revealed in the New Exodus redemption is God become flesh!* God the Son had to become flesh in order to be the ultimate Passover lamb (53:7), to bear the sin of many (53:12) as a substitutionary sacrifice. The Arm "bearing iniquity" (cf. 53:5, 6, 11) is the revelation of Yahweh's glory proclaimed in Exodus 34:6-7.

The apostles John and Paul both quoted Isaiah 53:1 in contexts that equated the Arm of Yahweh with Jesus (Jn. 12:38, Rom. 10:16). This section of Isaiah is so significant for our understanding of Jesus' identity and mission that it will be examined in depth in

---

46. *Isaiah*, 427.

Part Five, The Servant (Lord willing). For now, we rest our case that Isaiah 52-53 prophesied the coming of the God-Man.

Daniel 7. The prophecy of the coming of "one like a son of man" is so essential to the New Testament understanding of Jesus that we will treat it thoroughly in *Part Three, The Son of God and Son of Man* (Lord willing).[47] But I would regret it if I did not teach here, minimally, the elements that so strikingly show the Messiah would be the God-Man. To Daniel, God revealed His answer to the providential progression of beastly kingdoms:

> DANIEL 7:13-14
> "I saw in the night visions,
>> and behold, with the clouds of heaven
>>> there came one like a son of man,
>> and he came to the Ancient of Days
>>> and was presented before him.
> [14]And to him was given dominion
>> and glory and a kingdom,
> that all peoples, nations, and languages
>> should serve him;
> his dominion is an everlasting dominion,
>> which shall not pass away,
> and his kingdom one
>> that shall not be destroyed.

The subject of Daniel's vision was not "a son of man," but "One *like* a son of man," hinting that there is more to this being than natural humanity. And clearly so, because He is seen riding on the clouds of heaven, something Scripture elsewhere says is only done by Yahweh (Ps. 104:3, Isa. 19:1). Then He came to the Ancient of Days, whose throne is comprised of fiery flames of judgment (7:9-10). Who would dare do that, except a holy being? Rather than being consumed by God's fire because of sinfulness, He was given authority, glory, and the Kingdom, so that all peoples should "serve" *Him!* The Aramaic word behind "serve" is used for

---

47. Until then, see the author's sermon and expanded notes, "The Son of Man and the Saints of the Most High," 2 Feb 2012 (ProjectOne28.com/Son_of_Man).

the religious service offered to a deity.[48] It appears earlier in Daniel about "serving" the idol of Nebuchadnezzar (3:12, 14, 18). NIV is not far off to translate is as "worship." In the book of Daniel, it is clear that only the one true God is worthy to be "served" (3:17, 28; 6:16, 20). Therefore, the "One like a son of man" must be divine. He is worthy to be obeyed and worshiped like God alone is worthy to be obeyed and worshiped. He is the Messianic God-Man.

Jesus' favorite title for Himself was "*the* Son of Man," alluding to this prophecy in Daniel 7.[49] He employed it in statements like, "The Son of Man has authority on earth to forgive sins" (Mk. 2:10, cf. v. 5). The Pharisees assumed He was blaspheming, "Who can forgive sins but God alone?" (2:7). But that was point: the Son of Man is God in flesh. At His mock trial, Jesus' claim to be the Son of Man from Daniel 7 secured His death sentence for blasphemy, proving that the Jewish leaders understood the divine nature of this figure (Mt. 26:64-66). But truly, all peoples should worship Jesus for this!

Malachi 3. Fittingly, we close this section with a prophecy that the Angel of Yahweh, who is Yahweh, would come:

> [1]"Behold, I send my messenger, and he will prepare the way before me. And the Lord whom you seek will suddenly come to his temple; and the messenger of the covenant in whom you delight, behold, he is coming, says Yahweh of hosts. [2]But who can endure the day of his coming, and who can stand when he appears? For he is like a refiner's fire and like fullers' soap. [3]He will sit as a refiner and purifier of silver, and he will purify the sons of Levi and refine them like gold and silver, and they will bring offerings in righteousness to Yahweh. [4]Then the offering of Judah and Jerusalem will be pleasing to Yahweh as in the days of old and as in former years. [5]Then I will draw near to you for judgment...."

---

48. Charles D. Isbell, *TWOT*, 1059.

49. More than any other title, more than 65 times in the Gospels (George Eldon Ladd, *A Theology of the New Testament*, Revised Edition, ed. Donald A. Hagner [Grand Rapids: Eerdmans, 1993], 144).

PROPHECIES OF MESSIAH AS GOD-MAN	
PSALM 45:6	"Your throne, O God, is forever and ever"
ISAIAH 7:14	virgin birth: "call His Name Immanuel"
ISAIAH 9:6	"a Child… called… Warrior God, Father of Eternity"
ISAIAH 40:3-5	"prepare the way of Yahweh… our God"
ISAIAH 35:2-6	"Behold, your God… will come and save you"
ISAIAH 52:10, 53:1	"Yahweh has bared His holy Arm…"
DANIEL 7:13-14	"with the clouds of heaven… One like a son of man"
ZECHARIAH 12:10	"look on Me, on Him whom they have pierced"
MALACHI 3:1-5	"the Lord… will suddenly come… the Angel"

Mark opened his Gospel with a compound quotation from Malachi 3:1 and Isaiah 40 to explain John the Baptist's ministry (1:2-3). In Matthew and Luke, Jesus quoted it as having pointed to John.[50] Although the apostle John does not quote this prophecy, it is probably why he included Jesus' cleansing of the temple at the *beginning* of His ministry, in fulfillment of the prophecy in Malachi 3:1 that the Lord "will *suddenly* come to His temple" in purifying judgment.[51] Again, if Yahweh prophesied that John would "prepare the way before Me," and Jesus suddenly came, then Jesus is Yahweh, the Adonai who spoke Malachi 3!

So interestingly, in Malachi 3, Yahweh shifts back and forth from "Me" to "He" to "I," reflecting distinctions and unity in the Godhead.[52] Yahweh will come in His Second Person, literally, "the Angel of the covenant, in whom you delight" (Mal. 3:1). We

---

50. Mt. 11:10, Lk. 7:27 (cf. Lk. 1:17, 76 and the lit., "before the face of His coming," Acts 13:24, alluding to the LXX of Mal. 3:1).

51. Jn. 2:13-24. Cf. Carson, *John*, 179. "Who can stand when He appears?" (Mal. 3:2) is alluded to in Rev. 6:17 because of "the wrath of the Lamb" at His second coming.

52. On pp. 111-112, we will see this same phenomenon in Zechariah 12:10.

see the Old Testament closes with a promise that the Angel who expounded the Name of the I AM and delivered His people at the original Exodus would come again.

Our look at these Old Testament prophecies has confirmed our belief that the Angel of Yahweh did not retire after the Old Testament. Rather, He was promised to come as the God-Man, Yahweh-in-Messiah. Therefore, the New Testament proclamation that the Man Jesus is Yahweh, though nearly unthinkable, actually aligns with the promises in the Hebrew Scriptures.

CHAPTER SIX

JESUS AS GOD IN THE GOSPELS

In the final two chapters, we will study the abundance of additional evidence in the New Testament that Jesus is Yahweh the Son. Some of it is blunt and obvious, but some is more subtle and requires attention to the Old Testament background. We will note, again,[1] the necessity of believing in Jesus' Godhood for salvation and true worship.

As God in His Conception through Birth

The angel Gabriel announced that the virgin-born Child should be called *Yeshua* ("Yahweh saves") because "*He Himself* will save His people from their sins" (Mt. 1:21, AT). Everyone knew Yahweh is the One who will save (e.g., Isa. 25:9), yet Gabriel said this Child is the One who will save, because this Child is Yahweh. Matthew informs us this fulfilled the promise in Isaiah 7:14 that Yahweh would be born of a virgin, *Immanuel*, God with us![2]

---

1. Jn. 8:24 (lit.), expounded on pp. 59-60.

2. Mt. 1:22-23, see pp. 82-84 for treatment of Isa. 7:14.

When the pregnant Mary visited her cousin Elizabeth, who was pregnant with John the Baptist, Elizabeth was filled with the Spirit (Lk. 1:41) and exclaimed, "And why is this granted to me that the mother of my *Lord* should come to me? For behold, when the sound of your greeting came to my ears, the baby in my womb leaped for joy" (1:43-44). The Greek for "Lord" (*kurios*) could be used as a polite address, like our "Sir,"[3] or to honor a leader, such as a king. Elizabeth may simply (wonderfully) have been expressing faith that the Baby in Mary's womb is the Messiah (maybe even echoing David's "my Lord" in Psalm 110:1).

It seems, though, that Luke wants his Gospel readers to see more, based on what he immediately and then closely thereafter reports. First, as John Frame writes, "Surely the leaping of baby John was a supernaturally evoked response, appropriate to a divine visitation...."[4] Indeed, it was promised that John would be filled with the Holy Spirit from the womb to be the forerunner *for Yahweh*.[5] This was the moment John began pointing to the preeminence of Jesus as Yahweh, through his mother, who was acting as his Spirit-inspired interpreter (see 1:41). Elizabeth's words were not merely her own, but the Spirit's, and *He* certainly knew the divine identity of Baby Jesus. Therefore, this is an instance in which we can unpack the full weight of *kurios* as the Greek substitution for *Yahweh*. The Baby Jesus is Elizabeth's "Lord" because He is her God. Infant, yet infinite![6] Secondly, this understanding is confirmed by what closely follows in Luke's Gospel.

In Luke 2:9-11 (AT), an angel appeared to the shepherds to announce Jesus' birth. Notice both the opening and closing uses of *kurios* ("Lord"):

---

3. E.g., Jn. 4:11, 15, 19 of Jesus by the Samaritan woman *before* belief; 12:21 *of Philip*.

4. *The Doctrine of God*, 653.

5. *Kurios* in Luke 1:17 alludes to "Yahweh of armies" in Malachi 3:1, and *kurios* in Luke 1:76 is standing in for the original Yahweh in Isa. 40:3-5, qtd. in Lk. 3:4.

6. Stephen J. Nichols paraphrased Charles Spurgeon as saying "at once infant and infinite" ("The Deity of Christ Today," in *The Deity of Christ*, 38). He may have been thinking of

And an angel of the, *Lord* stood before, them, and the, glory of the, *Lord* shone around them, and they feared with, great fear. [10]And the angel said to, them, "Do not be fearing, because, behold, I am evangelizing to, you great joy, which will be for, all the people, [11]because today a, savior was born for, you, who is Christ, the, *Lord,* in the, city of, David.

Not only is the Child the Christ, He is a Savior. Not only is the Child a Savior, He is the Lord, the One whose glory is shining around His angel! The Lord, Yahweh – God the Son now in flesh. Therefore, He is not a savior like in the time of Judges; He is not a created, independent third party. He is Yahweh Himself, as in Isaiah 43:11, "I, I am Yahweh, and besides Me there is no Savior."[7]

Christ, as Yahweh, deserved the worship of the magi (Mt. 2:2, 11). They traveled perhaps about eight hundred miles over forty days to worship[8] a Baby, not waiting to be coronated, but already King of the Jews (2:2). The God-Child, at once infant and infinite.

---

the sermon titled "The Condescension of Christ": "And now wonder, ye angels, the Infinite has become an infant; he, upon whose shoulders the universe doth hang, hangs at his mother's breast…" (spurgeon.org/resource-library/sermons/).

7. Cf. "horn of salvation" in Lk. 1:69 with Yahweh in 2 Sam. 22:3, Ps. 18:2. Cf. also the NT verses designating Jesus "our God and Savior" (p. 125). Bowman and Komoszewski write, "In the context of the Old Testament religious and theological tradition, such a claim for Jesus [Savior, having just qtd. Heb. 5:9] is every bit as much an indication of deity as the claim that he made the universe. A heavenly or supernatural being to whom one looked as the source of deliverance or salvation is by definition one's God" (Robert M. Bowman, Jr., and J. Ed Komoszewski, *Putting Jesus in His Place: The Case for the Deity of Christ* [Grand Rapids, MI: Kregel, 2007], 209-210).

8. The Greek verb *proskuneō* could mean worship as to a deity or reverential homage paid to a human king (surely what Herod meant in 2:8). Carson writes, "Their own statement suggests homage paid royalty rather than the worship of Deity. But Matthew, having already told of the virginal conception, doubtless expected his readers to discern something more – viz., that the Magi 'worshiped' better than they knew" (*Matthew*, 86). Osborne writes, "… the latter ['worship' in the narrow sense] does fit here, and Matthew certainly wants the reader to think of worship" (*Matthew*, 87). Gathercole: "Even if such expressions of devotion or obeisance cannot be straightforwardly read as offerings of the worship due to the one God [though Gathercole argued for more in Mt. 8:2], it is probably still correct to say that Matthew presents pre-Easter *proskynesis* as anticipating that which is offered to the risen Jesus" when His Godhood is even clearer (*The Preexistent Son*, 69). Bowman and Komoszewski (*Putting Jesus in His Place*, 38-40, 293-294, n. 5) make perhaps the best point: Jesus Himself asserted in His temptation by Satan that God alone must be the object of *proskuneō* (Mt. 4:10), so

As God in His Ministry

Eclipsing John. As noted in the section on Old Testament prophecies, all four Gospels quote Isaiah 40 and Malachi 3 to explain John the Baptist's preparation for Yahweh, who came as Jesus. "John is bearing witness concerning Him, and he has cried out, saying, 'This was ̣the One of ̣whom I said, "The ̣One ̣coming after me has become ahead of me, because He was first ̣with respect to ̣me"'" (Jn. 1:15, AT). In a peculiar Greek phrase, John did not say, "He was before me," but literally, "He was first ̣with respect to ̣me." John testified that Jesus was ahead of him, not merely in terms of time, but also of essence: Jesus is preeminent as God the Son.

Son of God and Son of Man. *Part Three* will detail the self-identification, opposition, and worship of Jesus as God's Son and the Son of Man. Having looked briefly at the Daniel 7 Son of Man in Chapter Five,[9] we simply recognize here that both titles ascribe Godhood to Jesus. "Like father, like son." If the father is human, the son is human. If the Father is divine, the Son is divine (e.g., Jn. 5:18).

Calling Peter. Jesus prefaced His call to discipleship for Peter and his partners by miraculously causing too many fish to swim into their nets (Lk. 5:1-7). Who controls fish? Yahweh. So, "when Simon Peter saw it, he fell down at Jesus' knees, saying, 'Depart from me, for I am a sinful man, O Lord'" (5:8). This mirrors Isaiah's response to the presence of Yahweh (the pre-incarnate Jesus).[10] Peter, too, sensed that he was in the presence of the Holy One, and he feared that he would die in righteous judgment of his

---

Matthew is presenting 2:2 in light of that axiom. We also must read it in light of 14:33, 28:9, and 28:17, where it appears in its fullest, most appropriate sense.

9. Pp. 89-90.

10. Remember Jn. 12:41. Gathercole charts Joel Green's point of the correspondence between Lk. 5:1-11 and Isa. 6 at four stages in each narrative: epiphany, reaction, reassurance, commission (75, citing *The Gospel of Luke* [Grand Rapids, MI: Eerdmans, 1997], 233).

sinfulness. But Yahweh-in-flesh showed mercy and called him to the new occupation of catching His people (just as Yahweh said *He* would in Jer. 16:16).

Having come from heaven. Jesus repeatedly claimed to be Yahweh in His "I AM" sayings, which were clear enough to merit a blasphemy charge from the unbelieving, as we saw in Chapter Four. There we also came across Jesus' blunt statements in John 6 that He came down to earth from heaven.[11] He claimed to be Yahweh who came down to give eternal life to everyone in the world who believes into Him as their substitutionary sacrifice.

The Synoptic Gospels also present us with ten sayings concerning Jesus' coming from heaven to earth.[12] The first category illuminates the startling fact that the ones with most spontaneous and accurate understanding of Jesus' identity at the beginning of His ministry were demons. While Jesus was teaching in the synagogue in Capernaum, a demon cried out from within a possessed man, "What have you to do with us, Jesus of Nazareth? Have you come to destroy us? I know who you are – the Holy One of God" (Mk. 1:24, par. Lk. 4:34, cf. Mt. 8:29). This demon recognized Jesus as the Son of God who had presided over their exile from heaven thousands of years earlier. Jesus did not begin in Mary's womb; He existed in heaven as God before becoming the God-Man. This demon knew that and feared the judgment that the God-Man was ordained to execute upon not only him, but also on all the demons ("us," 1:24).

In a second category, Jesus spoke six distinct "I have come" sayings followed by His purpose for coming. The purpose clauses sum up His life's work. Simon Gathercole's thorough research has shown that this combination was not used of ordinary humans in ancient Jewish literature, but it closely matches statements of angels who previously existed in heaven and visited the earthly realm for

---

11. See page 49. Cf. Jn. 1:9, 3:31, 8:14, 9:39, 10:10, 11:27, 16:27, 28, 30, 17:8.

12. Gathercole, *The Preexistent Son*, 84.

a specific mission.[13] Therefore, the "I have come" plus purpose formula, in its most natural reading, implies Jesus' preexistence in heaven before birth on earth, because He possessed a will and exercised a choice to come to earth for reasons that He understood and embraced.

Whereas the formula itself presupposes preexistence, the content of the purpose clauses distinguish Jesus from created angels and humans, identifying Him as God. Jesus declared that He came to evangelize the gospel of the kingdom, to call sinners to repentance, to fulfill the Law and the Prophets, to Himself be the dividing line of all humanity, and to cast fire onto the earth.[14]

The goal of the Law and Prophets is *God*, manifesting the glory of His kingdom over all the earth to the everlasting joy of His people.[15] Jesus must be God to be the One who fulfills the whole of Hebrew Scripture. What is more, for this fulfillment, the enemies of God must first be destroyed. Jesus claimed He came to cast the fire of His judgment upon the earth,[16] like He did in foreshadow upon Sodom and Gomorrah – Jesus is the Yahweh of Genesis 19:24. Indeed, because the revelation of God's glory in Jesus was so sufficient in His first coming, "it will be more tolerable on the day of judgment for the land of Sodom than for" the townspeople who rejected Him (Mt. 11:24). Now the division of humanity between those who are devoured by fire or saved from it is determined by hatred or love for Jesus, just as it was determined in the Old Testament by hatred or love for Yahweh,[17] because Jesus is Yahweh in flesh. Therefore, because of the preexistence formula and especially the content, Jesus' "I have come" statements, even in the earlier Synoptic Gospels, are claims to be the eternal God who became the God-Man.

---

13. *Ibid.*, 110, 113-147.

14. Mk. 1:38, 2:17, 5:17; Mt. 9:13, 10:34, 35; Lk. 4:43, 5:32, 12:49, 51

15. See *Part One*, as well as *The Kingdom of God* (both free at ProjectOne28.com).

16. Lk. 12:49, cf. Mt. 3:11; 2 Pet. 3:7, 12

17. Ex. 20:5-6, Deut. 7:9-10, 30:15-20; Mt. 6:24, 10:37-39, 12:30

Thus Saith Yahweh vs. I Say. All other prophets borrow authority from God, "Thus saith Yahweh…." Jesus, though, did not preface His teachings in the standard way. In the Sermon on the Mount, for example, Jesus repeatedly said, "You have heard that it was said [in the Scriptures]… but *I say* to you…" (e.g., Mt. 5:21-22). Jesus was not replacing, contradicting, or changing the Scriptures; He was asserting the authority to interpret and apply the heart of the Scriptures. Combine this with the fact that Jesus "went up on the mountain" to reveal His commands (Mt. 5:1), and we see that He was acting like Yahweh on Sinai. Jesus could expound God's commands in Matthew 5 because He was the One who first spoke them in Exodus 20. Jesus is more than a new Moses; He is the God of Moses.

Jesus also often said, "Amen, amen, I am saying to you…."[18] Prefacing a statement with "amen" was an oath of truthfulness. It was doubled in Numbers 5:22 in the seriousness of life or death, to be confirmed by God or cursed by Him. Insight into Jesus' usage of, "Amen, amen," comes through the Pharisees' challenge of His, "*Egō eimi* the light of the world":

> [13]Therefore, the Pharisees said ˌtoˌ Him, "You yourself are bearing witness about yourself; your witness is not true." [14]Jesus answered and said ˌtoˌ them, "Even if I Myself am bearing witness about Myself, My witness is true, because I know where I came from, and where I am going away; but you yourselves do not know where I come from or where I am going away. [15]You yourselves are judging according to the flesh; I Myself am judging ˌabsolutelyˌ no one. [16]Yet even if I Myself judge, My judgment is true, because I am not alone, but I and the Father ˌwhoˌ sent Me. [17]And even in your law, it has been written that the witness ˌofˌ two men is true. [18]I AM the ˌoneˌ bearing witness about Myself, and the Father ˌwhoˌ sent Me is bearing witness about *Me*" (Jn. 8:13-18, AT).

The first, "Amen," was Jesus' witness, which counted because Jesus came from heaven in the presence of God the Father. The

Pharisees looked only at Jesus' flesh and concluded that He was merely a human teacher, and a false one at that. But Jesus' second, "Amen," was the Father's confirmation of His Son's truthfulness. Jesus voiced them both because the Father dwelled in Him.

> "You are believing that I am in the Father, and the Father is in *Me*, are you not?[19] The words which I Myself am saying to you I am not speaking from Myself, but the Father abiding in *Me* is doing His works. [11]Be believing Me that I am in the Father, and the Father in *Me;* and if not, be believing on account of the works themselves" (14:10-11, AT).

God is "the God of Amen" (Isa. 65:16, AT), and Jesus is God, "the Amen" (Rev. 3:14), the One in whom the fullness of God dwells. We can believe His words at least on account of His works.

Forgiving Sins. Jesus meant for His miracles to confirm His Godhood (Jn. 5:36, 10:32, 14:11). Once, so many gathered at the home where He was staying in Capernaum that there was no room to get in to hear Him proclaiming the word. Four men carried their paralyzed friend on a cot up onto the roof, removed a section, and lowered him down to Jesus.

> And when Jesus saw their faith, he said to the paralytic, "Son, your sins are forgiven." [6]Now some of the scribes were sitting there, questioning in their hearts, [7]"Why does this man speak like that? He is blaspheming! Who can forgive sins but God alone?" [8]And immediately Jesus, perceiving in his spirit that they thus questioned within themselves, said to them, "Why do you question these things in your hearts? [9]Which is easier, to say to the paralytic, 'Your sins are forgiven,' or to say, 'Rise, take up your bed and walk'?" (Mk. 2:5-9).

It was easier to say, "Your sins are forgiven," because who could know if it was true or not? On the other hand, if someone said, "Rise and walk," it would become immediately evident whether

---

18. Lit., Jn. 1:51, 3:3, 5, 11, 5:19, 24, 25, 6:26, 32, 8:34, 51, 58, etc.

19. Asked of His disciples with οὐκ ("not"), signaling the expectation of a positive answer.

or not he possessed the authority to say such a thing. Though forgiving sins was more difficult to *do*, it was easier to *say*. And when Jesus said it, it sounded like blasphemy to the scribes. If the paralytic sinned against Jesus, then Jesus could say, "I forgive you." But in a greater sense, all of the paralytic's sins were against God because they were rebellion against his Creator's will.[20] Therefore, the only One who can truly forgive all of a person's sins is God. Jesus could say such a thing, righteously, only if He was indeed God in flesh. So Jesus gave them a reason to trust Him:

> "But that you may know that the Son of Man has authority on earth to forgive sins" – he said to the paralytic – [11]"I say to you, rise, pick up your bed, and go home." [12]And he rose and immediately picked up his bed and went out before them all, so that they were all amazed and glorified God, saying, "We never saw anything like this!" (Mk. 2:10-12).

The miracle validated Jesus' claim to be the God of forgiveness.

Saving and Showing Mercy. Gathercole notes, "Jesus is frequently addressed as 'lord' in contexts when these speakers express not only Jesus' superiority to themselves, but also his power over their *circumstances* (8.2, 8, 25; 14.28)."[21] Also, "Matthew includes a number of sayings which tap into the invocations 'Lord, save,' and 'Lord, have mercy,' which are found most commonly in LXX Psalms" addressed to the *Kurios*, Yahweh.[22]

Calming the Storm. Once, having told His disciples, "Let us go across to the other side" of the sea (Mk. 4:35), a great windstorm caused waves to break into the boat, filling it with water. Surprisingly, Jesus was asleep on a cushion in the stern (4:38). In a story that will demonstrate His deity, this element highlights His humanity. God never sleeps (Ps. 121:4), but Jesus, as a Man, slept.

---

20. See Ps. 51:4; 2 Sam. 12:13; Gen. 20:6, 39:9; 1 Cor. 8:12. Cf. the event in Lk. 7:48-49.

21. *The Preexistent Son*, 245.

22. *Ibid.*, 246. Gathercole then lists LXX references, but I here list English versification: save, Ps. 12:1, 106:47, 118:25 [cf. "Hosanna!" in Mt. 21:9, 15], Mt. 8:25, 14:30; have mercy, Ps. 6:4, 30:10, 41:4, 41:10, 86:3, 123:3, Mt. 15:22, 17:15, 20:30, 20:31.

Two natures – human and divine – were distinct but united in the One Person of Jesus.[23] The Godhood of Jesus, in the spiritual realm, did not sleep, but He slept in His Manhood.

> …And they woke him and said to him, "Teacher, do you not care that we are perishing?" ["Save us, *Lord!*" (Mt. 8:25)] [39]And he awoke and rebuked the wind and said to the sea, "Peace! Be still!" And the wind ceased, and there was a great calm. [40]He said to them, "Why are you so afraid? Have you still no faith?" [41]And they were filled with great fear and said to one another, "Who then is this, that even the wind and the sea obey him?" (Mk. 4:38-41).

Jesus had said, "Let us go across to the other side," so they should have trusted His presence to keep them safe until His word was fulfilled. But they feared the waves – and yet, even after the waves calmed down, they were "filled with *great* fear" in a response to God's presence in Christ. They asked, "What sort of man is this, that even winds and sea obey him?" (Mt. 8:27). No ordinary man. The Gospel writers left off the answer for literary effect, clearly expecting readers to supply the truth from the Old Testament. Psalm 107 taught that Yahweh commands the stormy winds and waves:

> [28]Then they cried to Yahweh in their trouble,
>   and He delivered them from their distress.
> [29]He made the storm be still,
>   and the waves of the sea were hushed.

The Jesus of Mark 4 is the Yahweh of Psalm 107.[24] Revere Him! Cry to Him for salvation!

Prophecy in His Name. Jesus said, on judgment day, "Many will say to Me, 'Lord, Lord, did we not prophesy *in your name*, and cast out demons in your name, and do many mighty works

---

23. See the text of the Chalcedonian Definition of 451 A.D. with commentary in Wayne Grudem, *Systematic Theology* (Grand Rapids, MI: Zondervan, 1994), 556-563.

24. See more depth about the God-Man subduing the chaotic effects of the enemy in *Light Shines in the Darkness* (free at ProjectOne28.com).

in your name?'" (Mt. 7:22). The emphatic, doubled address of *kurios* strengthens the allusion to Deuteronomy 18:20,[25] in which Yahweh said, "But the prophet who presumes to speak a word *in my name* that I have not commanded him to speak... that same prophet shall die." Jesus declared that unbelievers will presume to prophesy in His Name because He is Yahweh incarnate.

Bridegroom. A frequent and powerful metaphor in the Hebrew Scriptures portrayed Yahweh as Israel's bridegroom or husband.[26] The commandments at Sinai were like wedding vows.[27] In Israel's idolatry, she broke the covenant and committed spiritual adultery against Yahweh.[28] Through the prophets Isaiah and Hosea, Yahweh officially divorced Israel for her infidelity (Isa. 54:6-8, cf. Jer. 3:8). Yet the promise of the New Covenant included Yahweh again speaking tenderly to win His wayward bride:

> And in that day, declares Yahweh, you will call me "My Husband".... And I will betroth you to me forever. I will betroth you to me in righteousness and in justice, in steadfast love and in mercy. I will betroth you to me in faithfulness. And you shall know Yahweh.[29]

> ... and as the bridegroom rejoices over the bride,
>   so shall your God rejoice over you.[30]

In that Jewish context, when Jesus called Himself the bridegroom, He claimed to be the fulfillment of Yahweh coming to remarry His people.[31] John the Baptist also proclaimed his joy that Jesus had come as the bridegroom (Jn. 3:29). The apostles

---

25. Gathercole, *The Preexistent Son*, 67-68; Peterson, "Toward a Systematic Theology of the Deity of Christ," in *The Deity of Christ*, 197.

26. E.g., Isa. 54:5

27. Ezek. 16:8-14

28. Jer. 31:32, Ezek. 16:15 ff., esp. vv. 32, 38.

29. Hos. 2:14-16, 19-20

30. Isaiah 54:4-5; cf. with Isaiah the Servant, who is identified with Yahweh (Isa. 53:1) and is prophesied to fulfill this salvation/marriage (61:10).

31. Mk. 2:19, Mt. 22:2, 25:5

Paul and John continued the use of this metaphor that identified Jesus with Yahweh.[32] At His return, the Church will experience the ultimate love, faithfulness, provision, protection, and joy to which human marriage serves as a parable.

Owning Angels. Jesus referred to the angels as "His angels" because He is God, and they obey Him when He sends them (Mt. 13:41, 49; 24:31; Rev. 1:1).[33]

Owning the Sabbath. One of first things Jesus did (and repeatedly did) to put Himself on the Pharisees' hit list was "breaking" the Sabbath with His methods of healing and itinerant living. Not only that, but He commanded others to "break" the Sabbath (for example, the paralytic who obeyed by carrying his cot home in John 5:10). To appreciate the significance, we must understand that Yahweh prescribed the death penalty for anyone who violated the Sabbath.[34] The exile lasted seventy years to correspond with the number of Sabbatical years spurned,[35] and the return from exile to establish the kingdom of God was promised for those who kept the Sabbath (Isa. 58:13). The Pharisees correctly cared so much for this law! But, just as they built man-made traditions around speaking the Name and supporting their parents, they also went beyond what is written regarding rest from work on the Sabbath. They classified thirty-nine different kinds of prohibited "work,"[36] many of which missed the point that the Sabbath was given to be a break from regular work done for provision, trusting that Yahweh is their provider. The lack of mercy in their hearts angered Jesus,[37] and He did not stop or retreat in His responses to their charges.

---

32. 2 Cor. 11:2, Rom. 7:1-4, Eph. 5:25-32, Rev. 19:7-9, 21:2, 9

33. Stephen J. Wellum, "The Deity of Christ in the Synoptic Gospels," in *The Deity of Christ*, 83, n. 61, quoting Robert L. Reymond, *Jesus, Divine Messiah: The New and Old Testament Witness* (Ross-shire, Scotland: Mentor, 2003), 216.

34. Ex. 20:9-10, 31:15, 35:2

35. Lev. 26:34-35, 43; 2 Chron. 36:21

36. Carson, *John*, 244.

37. Mk. 3:5, cf. Lk. 13:15

In fact, He doubled-down: "the Son of Man is Lord even of the Sabbath" (Mk. 2:28, cf. Mt. 12:8, Lk. 6:5). John Frame explains:

> In the Old Testament, the Sabbath is the day that Yahweh claims for himself, over against all human interests: "[…] but the seventh day is a Sabbath to the LORD your God" (Ex. 20:9-10). It is holy to him (vv. 8, 11). So through Isaiah, God chastised the people for "doing as you please on my holy day" (Isa. 58:13). The Sabbath belongs to the Lord alone and not to any man. But in Mark 2:28, Jesus claims lordship over it. Clearly this use of *kyrios* is a claim to deity.[38]

Owning the Elect, Building His Assembly. It is unfortunate that English traditionally mistranslates "church" through *kurioikos*, "the Lord's house," rather than from the actual *ekklēsia*, which means "assembly."[39] *Ekklēsia* was regularly used in the Septuagint of the Old Testament people of God. Therefore, when Jesus promised to build *His* Assembly (Mt. 16:18), He revealed that He is the God of the Old Testament, the God of one Assembly united across the ages in Him (cf. Heb. 12:23).

Jesus began building by calling to Himself twelve disciples, representative of the twelve tribes of Israel, sent out to regather the lost sheep of the house of Israel.[40] Jesus was reconstituting a New Israel. And He is not one of the Twelve.[41] He is not just a part of New Israel. He is the Lord of New Israel. Therefore, when He adds the full number of Gentiles and pours a spirit of grace and supplication to turn Israel back,[42] completing His building process, then He will send "*his* angels… and they will gather *his* elect from the four winds" (Mt. 24:31). God's chosen people are Jesus' chosen people because Jesus is God the Son, their Savior, and He chooses them in concert with the Father, which we see next.

---

38. *The Doctrine of God*, 654.

39. D. W. B. Robinson, "Church," in *New Bible Dictionary* (Downers Grove, IL: Inter-Varsity Press, 1996), 199.

40. Mt. 10:6, 19:28; cf. Eph. 2:11-22, 1 Pet. 2:9-10, Gal. 6:16, Rev. 7:4-8

41. Gathercole, *The Preexistent Son*, 55-57.

Knowing Infinitely, Governing Absolutely, Saving Infallibly. In Matthew 11, Jesus made a series of staggering statements:

> I thank you, Father, Lord of heaven and earth, that you have hidden these things from the wise and understanding and revealed them to little children; [26]yes, Father, for such was your gracious will. [27]All things have been handed over to me by my Father, and no one knows the Son except the Father, and no one knows the Father except the Son and anyone to whom the Son chooses to reveal him. [28]Come to me, all who labor and are heavy laden, and I will give you rest. [29]Take my yoke upon you, and learn from me, for I am gentle and lowly in heart, and you will find rest for your souls (11:25-29).

First, Jesus revealed His exhaustive and meticulous sovereignty: "All things have been handed over to Me." Who is so worthy and able, but a Member of the Triune God? Then Jesus said He possesses infinite knowledge. B. B. Warfield explains the implications:

> The Son can be known only by the Father in all that He is, as if His being were infinite and as such inscrutable to the finite intelligence; and His knowledge alone – again as if He were infinite in His attributes – is competent to compass the depths of the Father's infinite being. He who holds this relation to the Father cannot conceivably be a creature.[43]

Robert Reymond agrees that such a statement "lifts Jesus above the sphere of the ordinary mortal and places him in a position not of equality merely, but of absolute reciprocity and interpenetration of knowledge with the Father."[44] Jesus is infinite, so it requires the infinite knowledge of the Father to know Him as He is. Also, Jesus is infinite in His perfect knowing of the Father,[45] and no other can know the Father unless Jesus chooses to reveal Him, exercising sovereignty in salvation as only God can.

---

42. Respectively, Rom. 11:25-27 and Zech. 12:10–13:1, Rev. 1:7.

43. *The Lord of Glory* (repr. Grand Rapids, MI: Baker, 1974), 83, qtd. in Wellum, 82-83.

44. *Jesus, Divine Messiah*, 206-210, qtd. in Wellum, 82.

45. Osborne comments on the Greek behind "know," *epiginōskō*: "it is likely that there is a

Jesus closed with an invitation (Mt. 11:28-29) for all the weary to come to Him for refreshing as the Yahweh who promised in Jeremiah 31:25, "For I will satisfy the weary soul, and every languishing soul I will replenish."[46] The rest Jesus gives has been longed for since the days of Noah and promised in the end-time kingdom.[47] "[T]he words 'and you will find rest for your souls' are directly quoted from Jeremiah 6:16,"[48] spoken first by Yahweh and then again by Yahweh-in-flesh.

Jesus also spoke with similar themes in John 10:27-30 (AT):

> My sheep hear My voice, and I Myself know them, and they follow Me, [28]and I Myself give them eternal life, and they absolutely cannot perish into the age to come, and no one will seize them out of My hand. [29]My Father, who gave them to Me, is greater than all, and no one has power to seize them out of the hand of the Father. [30]I and the Father are One."

Jesus is the good shepherd and the source of eternal life as Yahweh the Son (fulfilling Ezek. 34). He praises His Father as greater than all, and then asserts Oneness with the Father, meaning that He, too, is greater than all. Indeed, His sheep are safe in His hand and His Father's hand, which are distinct yet united in essence and mission. As in John 8:58-59, the Jewish leaders clearly hear Jesus' claim to Godhood, but respond in unbelief (10:31-33, AT):

> The Jews again bore stones, in order that they may stone Him. [32]Jesus answered them, "I showed you many good works from the Father. On account of which work of them are you going to stone *Me?*" [33]The Jews answered Him, "We are not going to stone you concerning a good work, but concerning blasphemy, and because *you,* being a man, are making yourself God!"

---

perfective force in the prefix ἐπί – with the meaning 'know exactly, completely, through and through' (*BAGD*, 291)" (*Matthew*, 440).

46. Wellum, 83, n. 59; Carson, *Matthew*, 278.

47. *Noah* sounds like the Hebrew for *rest* (Gen. 5:28-29; cf. 2:1-3, Ps. 95:7-11, Heb. 3:7–4:11).

48. Carson, *Matthew*, 278.

The other possibility is that Jesus is not merely a Man and is not "making" Himself God; He truly has been and will be God for all eternity. He knows infinitely, governs absolutely, and saves His sheep infallibly.

Making Mud. This miracle, one of Jesus' Sabbath healings, probably qualifies as His strangest. Why did Jesus, in John 9:1-7, choose to heal the man born blind by spitting on the dirt, making mud, pasting it on his eyes, and telling him to go wash in the Pool of Siloam, which means "Sent"?

One reason might have been to intentionally violate the Pharisees' tradition that it was unlawful on the Sabbath to knead "dough" (the same Greek word as what Jesus' made from the dirt). He may have been pushing their buttons to ensure His death. A second reason may be as a necessary precursor to the man washing in the Pool called Sent. Southwest of Jerusalem, living water was sent to the pool via a channel from the spring of Gihon in the Kidron Valley.[49] Washing in the pool called Sent would heal the man's blindness because Jesus is the Giver of the true Living Water, having been *sent* from heaven to earth by God the Father to be the Messiah! Jesus wanted everyone to learn that parable. The third and, I believe, ultimate reason: Jesus used mud to mirror what *He* did in Genesis 2:7, forming Adam's body from the dust.[50] Jesus made new eyes, as it were, for this blind man to demonstrate that He is Yahweh, the Creator. Isaiah 35 had promised that, when Yahweh comes, "the eyes of the blind shall be opened" unto a New Creation like a New Eden. Yahweh came as the God-Man, Jesus Christ, giving foretastes of the New Creation.

Being Worshiped. The formerly blind man was excommunicated from the synagogue for his bold testimony to Jesus before the Pharisees. After that, Jesus "found him" (Jn. 9:35, such grace). Jesus asked the man if he believed into the Son of Man (who was

---

49. Carson, *John*, 365.

50. So also many early church fathers (Carson, *John*, 363).

promised in Daniel 7). The man wanted to, but did not yet know for certain that Jesus is the Son of Man. When Jesus identified Himself, the formerly blind man said, *"'I am believing, Lord!' And he worshiped Him"* (9:38, AT). We noted earlier that faithful Jews protected the worship of God and were repulsed by even hints of idolatry, and yet the disciples earlier worshiped Jesus as the Yahweh of Job 9 who walks on waves and stops winds (Mt. 14:22-33). Here, this man, having benefited from Jesus' gracious power, worshiped Him as the divine Son of Man, the Lord. Jesus received this man's worship because it was right (the goal of Dan. 7:14).

Jesus also appropriated children's worship of Yahweh to Himself. After His triumphal entry, the children were singing, "Hosanna to the Son of David!" in the presence of the miracle-working Jesus and indignant chief priests and scribes (Mt. 21:15). They called on Jesus to stop the children, but Jesus replied: "Have you never read, 'Out of the mouth of infants and nursing babies you have prepared praise'?" (21:16). Jesus quoted Psalm 8:2 about the worship of *Yahweh* to validate worship of *Him* – which only works if He is Yahweh!

The Father purposes "that all may honor the Son, just as they honor the Father" (Jn. 5:23). If we do not honor Jesus as God the Son, then we are not honoring the Father either (5:23). Religious people who do not recognize the full Godhood of Jesus, eternal Son of the Father – no matter how pious and sincere – are not worshiping God in spirit and truth. Later we will see more instances of Jesus being worshiped after His resurrection.

Praying of Preexistent Glory. On the night of His betrayal, knowing His crucifixion, resurrection, and ascension had drawn near, Jesus prayed, "...and now, glorify Me Yourself, Father, with Yourself, with, the glory which I was having with You before the world was, to be" (Jn. 17:5, AT). Also:

> Father, whom You have given to Me, I am wanting that where
> I Myself am, those also may be with Me, in order they may see

> My glory, which You have given to Me because You loved Me
> before the founding of the world (17:24, AT).

Jesus existed for eternity before Creation as God the Son with God
the Father and Holy Spirit. How incredible to see His priority in
prayer: for us to be with Him and see His preexistent glory. May it
be so now, increasingly, and in perfect clarity at His return.[51] Come
quickly, Lord Jesus!

AS GOD CRUCIFIED

Jesus was rejected from being King by the Jewish leaders
just as He was during Samuel's time (1 Sam. 8:7). After the
false trial before the Sanhedrin and Pilate's cowardice before the
manipulators, Jesus was scourged and crucified. They pierced
His hands and feet, fulfilling Psalm 22, in between two sinners,
fulfilling Isaiah 53 about the Servant who is the Arm of Yahweh.[52]
The soldiers typically sped deaths by breaking their legs, so they
could not press up to get deep enough breaths while hanging from
the crosses.

> JOHN 19:33-37 (AT)
> But having come upon Jesus, when they saw Him having died
> already, they did not break His legs, [34]but one of the soldiers
> stabbed His side with a spear, and immediately blood and
> water came out. [35]And the one having seen has borne witness,
> and *his* witness is *true*, and that one knows he is speaking truly,
> in order that you yourselves may believe. [36]Because these things
> happened in order that the Scripture may be fulfilled: "Not a
> bone of His will be broken." [37]And again another Scripture is
> saying, "They will look upon whom they pierced."

The soldier, as a professional executioner, knew his responsibility
to ensure the convicts actually died. There could be no mistake, so
he pierced Jesus to be certain. The apostle John emphasized his
truthful witness to this, so that we may believe. How could this

---

51. A purpose for John's writing (1:14, 2:11). Cf. 2 Cor. 3:18, 1 Cor. 13:12; 1 Jn. 3:2.
52. Ps. 22:16 (Jesus qtd. 22:1 on the Cross, Mt. 27:46); Isa. 53:12 (qtd. in Lk. 22:37)

event help us believe? Verse 36 starts with, "Because." Jesus being pierced should lead us to faith because it happened to fulfill two specific Scriptures.

First, Exodus 12:46 contained the command for Israelites not to break any bones of the Passover lamb (cf. Num. 9:12). This Scripture, not originally a prophecy, pointed typologically to the ultimate Passover Lamb, the Servant of Isaiah 53, the Jesus introduced by the Baptist: "Behold, the Lamb of God who takes away the sin of the world!" (Jn. 1:29, 36). If the soldier had come any earlier, or if Jesus had died any later, then Jesus' legs would have been broken, and the typology of the Passover lamb would have been broken, too. But God providentially orchestrated the events of the crucifixion to fulfill the Scripture,[53] so that we can believe Jesus was not a victim, but a voluntary substitute to absorb our punishment, so He may *pass over* us in mercy!

The second Scripture quoted as fulfilled by Jesus' piercing is Zechariah 12:10, which is altogether astounding:

> And I will pour out on the house of David and the inhabitants of Jerusalem a spirit of grace and pleas for mercy, so that, when they look on me, on him whom they have pierced, they shall mourn for him, as one mourns for an only son, and weep bitterly over him, as one weeps over a firstborn.

Yahweh promised to give the grace of repentance "when they look on *Me*, on Him whom they have *pierced*"! The Hebrew word implies a fatal wound.[54] It appears in Zechariah 13:3 as the mode of the death penalty for sin and in Numbers 25:8 as the means of propitiation by a priest. In Zechariah 12:10 *Yahweh promised that He would be thus pierced!* John quoted this promise, so that we may believe that Jesus is Yahweh! And this enables us to understand why Jesus had said earlier, cryptically, "When you lift up the Son of Man, then you will know that I AM" (*egō eimi*, Jn. 8:28, AT).

---

53. Isa. 53:10, Lk. 22:22, Acts 2:23, 4:27-28

But how could the immortal Yahweh die? How could they fatally pierce One who is a Spirit? Only if God became a God-Man. God the Son became flesh in order to overcome His divine impossibility of dying as our substitutionary sacrifice (Heb. 2:14-15). This fits Zechariah's prophecy exactly. Notice the shift from the first person ("look on Me") to the third person ("on Him whom they have pierced"). The "on Him" cannot be separated from Yahweh, because it further describes "on Me."[55] Yet the "Me" cannot be pierced as a Spirit. The solution is the Trinity: the Father and Spirit remain unpierceable, but the Son took on flesh to be pierced. The Persons are distinct, but unified. *In Jesus, Yahweh was pierced, because Jesus is Yahweh the Son.* Therefore, it is more than a metaphor that the mourning will be "as one mourns for an only son" (Zech. 12:10). Jesus literally is the One-of-a-kind Son of God, and we grieve that our sins caused Him to be pierced.

Utterly essential for salvation is the truth in the doctrine of Christ's two natures, divine and human, distinct but inseparable in One Person. Only the Arm of Yahweh is strong enough to save.[56] No man can ransom another; only God can ransom.[57] Yet the ransom price must be paid: the penalty of death under the infinite wrath of God. God cannot die, and man cannot save – only the perfect God-Man can be the Mediator between the holy God and sinful mankind (1 Tim. 2:5). Only the God-Man can bear God's infinite wrath toward the sins of the world in Himself to satisfy God in His holiness and love.[58] Only the incorruptible God-Man can conquer corruption and defeat death by death. Only the God-

---

54. *ESV Study Bible*, 1767. See also Köstenberger, "The Deity of Christ in John's Gospel," in *The Deity of Christ*, 158.

55. The "Him" is connected to Zechariah 13:7, "'Awake, O sword, against My Shepherd, against the Man who stands next to Me,' declares Yahweh of hosts. 'Strike the shepherd, and the sheep will be scattered…',", through Jesus' quotation of it in Matthew 26:31, Mark 14:27. However, Carson's language that the "Him" of 12:10 refers to God's "representative, the Shepherd" (*John*, 627) could sound like an independent third party, especially absent an identification that does justice to the "look on *Me*." We must be clear that the Shepherd is Yahweh the Son.

56. Pp. 86-88. Cf. Isa. 43:11, 45:21, 59:1, 16, 63:5; Ps. 3:8, 62:1-2, 6; Jo. 2:9; Jas. 4:12.

Man can draw sinful humans into Himself, sanctify them, and transform them into partakers of the divine nature (2 Pet. 1:3-4, Rom. 8:29-30; 2 Cor. 3:18; 1 Jn. 3:2).[59] If Jesus Christ is not truly God and truly Man, then no one can be saved. But He is, and we can!

We come again to the apex of *Part One:* we most clearly see the glory of Yahweh in the crucifixion of the God-Man.[60] Yahweh had defined His glory as just and wrathful, loving and merciful, *bearing iniquity* (Ex. 34:6-7, AT). *Jesus bore our iniquities as Yahweh the Son, the Glory of God become flesh* to endure our deserved punishment in our place. *Looking on the pierced One is looking upon Yahweh* (Zech. 12:10, Jn. 19:37). Let us gaze upon His beauty and worship like the soldiers who said, "Truly this was the Son of God!" (Mt. 27:54).

As God Resurrected

Jesus had prophesied repeatedly that He would be raised on the third day.[61] His resurrection validated all of His teachings (1 Tim. 3:16), including the ones about Himself as the I AM. The resurrection proved that Jesus is God the Son (Rom. 1:4). Therefore, we continue to see Him speaking and acting like Yahweh and receiving the worship due to Yahweh alone.

---

57. Ps. 49:7-9, 15 (see p. 40)

58. Anselm, in *Cur Deus Homo?*, reasoned, "there is no-one... who *can* make this satisfaction except God himself.... but no-one *ought* to make it except man... it is necessary that one who is God-man should make it" (2.6). And, "It is needful that the very same Person who is to make this satisfaction be perfect God and perfect man, since no-one *can* do it except one who is truly God, and no-one *ought* to do it except one who is truly man" (2.7, qtd. in John R. W. Stott, *The Cross of Christ*, 20th Anniv. Ed. [Downers Grove, IL: IVP Books, 2006], 120, emphasis his).

59. Athanasius, *De Synodis* 51 (ccel.org/ccel/schaff/npnf204.xxii.ii.iii.html), to which I was pointed by Rob Lister, *God Is Impassible and Impassioned: Toward a Theology of Divine Emotion* (Wheaton, IL: Crossway, 2013), 83 (cf. Frame, 733; Grudem, 553).

60. See *Part One*, 54-56 (free at ProjectOne28.com/glory).

61. Mt. 12:39-40, 16:21, 17:22-23, 20:18-19 (cf. 26:61, 27:39-40, 62-65; Mk. 8:31, 9:31, 10:32-34 (cf. 14:58, 15:29-30); Lk. 9:22, 18:31-33 (cf. 24:6-7, 44-47).

When the resurrected Jesus intercepted the women running back from the empty tomb, "they came up and took hold of his feet and *worshiped* him" (Mt. 28:9). Jesus did not rebuke them because He was worthy of it as God the Son.

Later, Jesus teleported into the disciples' locked room, pronounced peace, and showed them His hands *and side* as proof of His bodily resurrection. "Therefore, the disciples rejoiced, having beheld *the Lord*" (Yahweh, Jn. 20:20, AT, cf. 1:14). Jesus commissioned them, "And having said this, He breathed upon them and is saying, 'Receive the Holy Spirit'" (20:22, AT). Jesus' breathing reenacted the Creation of Adam in Genesis 2:7, demonstrating that Jesus is the Creator, the Spirit of God is His Spirit, and He is recreating a new species of Man in His image.[62]

Thomas missed the first appearance and refused to believe without physical verification (Jn. 20:24-25). Eight days later, Jesus teleported in again, pronounced peace, and mercifully offered His hands *and side* to Thomas (20:26-27). "Thomas answered and said to Him, *'My Lord and my God!'* (20:28, AT). Thomas' worshipful declaration of faith is the last event before John's purpose statement for his Gospel. In response, Jesus promised happiness for all who believe even without seeing (20:29). In such a position, Thomas' worship forms the narrative peak in the Gospel,[63] the climax and goal for John's writing: that we all would share Thomas' adoration of Jesus as the Lord God, *Yahweh Elohim*.

The disciples met Jesus again on the mountain in Galilee. "And when they saw him, *they worshiped him*, but some doubted" (Mt. 28:17).

> Even though Matthew's narrative is characteristically concise, many believe that more than the Eleven apostles were present at this event. Back in Jerusalem, the women were running to

---

62. Creator (Jn. 1:1-3), His Spirit (Acts 16:7, Rom. 8:9), New Man (1 Cor. 15:47, Eph. 2:15)

63. Köstenberger, "The Deity of Christ in John's Gospel," in *The Deity of Christ*, 107.

tell Jesus' disciples (28:8), a group obviously larger than the Eleven.[64] Jesus commanded them to tell His "brothers" to meet Him in Galilee (28:10). Again, more than the Eleven were His brothers.[65] The view that many other disciples were present also helps make more sense of the report that "some doubted" (28:17). It is difficult to think that some of the Eleven doubted in Galilee, because they all had already seen the resurrected Jesus in Jerusalem (most of them more than once) and worshiped Him there. Therefore, it is best to interpret this as an appearance to the Eleven and many more.[66]

Either the others hesitated because "they disbelieved for joy" (as in Luke 24:41), because of initial uncertainty whether it was really the same Jesus, or because of uncertainty about worshiping a man as God (which would underscore the earlier point about Jewish sobriety on this issue). Either way, the inclusion of this hiccup in the climax of Matthew's Gospel demonstrates his care to report the facts faithfully. And it also encourages us not to be among the doubters, but the true worshipers.

Then, as if to assure the crowd of disciples that worshiping Him is appropriate, Jesus asserted all authority in heaven and earth as the divine Son of Man (Mt. 28:18).[67] He commanded His disciples to disciple all the people groups, "baptizing them into the Name of the Father and of the Son and of the Holy Spirit" (28:19, AT). In one of the clearest Trinitarian formulas, Jesus is equal in essence with the Father and the Holy Spirit, and the Three Persons comprise only One Name. Yahweh is Father, Son, and Spirit.

Therefore, disciple-making includes "teaching them to be keeping as much as all I commanded you..." (28:20, AT). The

---

64. See the difference in Lk. 6:13; note also 6:17. Compare Mt. 13:10 with Mk. 4:10.

65. Mt. 12:48-50

66. Sam McVay, Jr., and Spencer Stewart, *Introduction to Disciple-making: Obeying the Global Mandate of the Resurrected King Jesus* (El Dorado, KS: Project one28, 2013), 11 (free at ProjectOne28.com/i2dm). Cf. Carson, *Matthew*, 594.

67. For the allusions to Dan. 7:13-14 in Mt. 28:18, *Introduction to Disciple-making*, 13-14. On the assurance in context of 28:17, *Putting Jesus in His Place*, 39.

language of keeping commands comes from Yahweh on Mount Sinai.[68] On this *mount* in Galilee, Jesus reiterated Himself as Yahweh in flesh. He deserves absolute obedience as our covenant Lord.

Finally, He said, "And behold, I Myself am with you all the days until the completion of the age" (28:20, AT). For the second time in Matthew's Gospel, Jesus claimed eternal omnipresence (being present everywhere), an attribute possessed only by Yahweh.[69]

Jesus is God, and after the resurrection, all the disciples knew it. At Pentecost, Peter preached that *Jesus* pouring out His Spirit fulfilled Joel's promise of *Yahweh* pouring out His Spirit, because Jesus is both Christ and *Lord*, Yahweh.[70] Peter assured that everyone who repents of his sinfulness and calls upon the Name of Jesus (as the Yahweh of Joel 2:32) will receive His Spirit (Acts 2:37-41).

"Hallelu*jah!* What a Savior!"[71]

---

68. Exodus 20:6, cf. 15:26, 16:28; Lev. 22:31, 26:3; Dt. 4:2, 4:40, 5:10, 5:29, 6:2, 6:17.

69. Mt. 18:20, Ps. 139:7-12, Jer. 23:23-24, Acts 17:28, cf. Col. 1:17

70. Acts 2:16-21 (quoting Joel 2:28-32), 2:33, 36

71. This is the title of a hymn by Philip P. Bliss (cyberhymnal.org/htm/h/a/halwasav.htm). *Hallelujah* means, "Praise Yah!" (a shortened form of Yahweh).

CHAPTER SEVEN

JESUS AS GOD
IN THE APOSTOLIC WRITINGS

The apostolic writings contain numerous quotations, allusions, and descriptions of Jesus as the *kurios* (Yahweh) of the Old Testament, as well as nine passages which call Jesus *theos* ("God") in relationship with God the Father and Spirit.

AS *THEOS* (GOD)

The apostle John opened his Gospel with an allusion to Genesis 1:1, teaching that Jesus existed before the beginning as the Creator of all things, who then became flesh to accomplish the promised New Creation.[1]

JOHN 1:1
In the beginning was the Word, and the Word was with God, and the Word was God.

A word is an expression of a mind, a thought, a will. After surveying the Old Testament categories of God's "word," D. A.

---

1. Jn. 1:1-3. For the New Creation theme, see Jn. 1:4, 12-14; 2:1-11, 3:1-8; Carson, *John*, 113, 168, 175.

Carson summarized, "In short, God's 'Word' in the Old Testament is his powerful self-expression in creation, revelation, and salvation...."[2] God is so infinitely perfect and lively that His Self-expression is not just sound waves, but an infinitely perfect and lively Person: His eternally co-existent, co-equal Son! The second clause ("and the Word was with God") represents the Word as a distinct Person in relationship with God the Father. (Remember how we saw *Elohim* use the plural "Us" and "Our" and the Angel of Yahweh as Yahweh in relationship with Yahweh.[3]) The third clause ("and the Word was God") clarifies that the Word is not some created thing. He is God. God with God. Father and Son.

The *New World Translation* of the Jehovah's Witnesses infamously renders John 1:1c as, "and the Word was a god." They claim this is correct because the original Greek has no definite article ("the") before "God," so it must be indefinite ("a"), one god among many gods. Their fuller theology teaches that Jesus was the archangel Michael, the first created being, who later became a man.[4] Either of two points can refute this blasphemy, the first dealing with the Greek of John 1:1, and the second more simply reading the English in context.

Jehovah's Witnesses grossly misrepresent Greek grammar by claiming that the lack of a definite article automatically means the reference is indefinite. (Ninety-four percent of the time, they violate their own claim.[5]) In truth, New Testament Greek often omitted the article before a definite noun for numerous reasons.[6] In other words, even without the definite article, a noun is often *not* indefinite.

---

2. *John*, 216. E.g., Ps. 33:6 (Creation); Isa. 38:4 (revelation); Ps. 107:17-20 (salvation).

3. See pp. 63-64 and 65-70.

4. Matt Slick, "Jehovah's Witnesses' Beliefs" (carm.org/jehovahs-witnesses-beliefs).

5. R. H. Countess, *The Jehovah's Witnesses' New Testament: A Critical Analysis of the* New World Translation *of the Christian Greek Scriptures* (Phillipsburg, NJ: P&R, 1982), 54, qtd. in Wallace, *Greek Grammar Beyond the Basics*, 267.

6. Wallace catalogues "at least ten constructions in which a noun may be definite though

Often the article is given to the subject (here: *ho logos*, "the Word") but not to the predicate nominative in order to distinguish the two parts of speech.[7] The lack of the article before *theos* ("God") is how we know *not* to translate, "and God was the Word." Since the definite "God" in 1:1b refers to the Father, such a mistranslation of 1:1c would suggest the Father is the Word (the heresy of modalism). That would contradict 1:1b that the Word is a distinct Person in relationship "with God" the Father.

The Greek word order of John 1:1c fits Colwell's Construction: the predicate nominative (*theos*) precedes the "to be" verb and lacks the article. Most frequently, by far, Colwell's Construction is used to emphasize the essence of the subject. In other words, a pre-verbal predicate nominative without the article is almost always qualitative.[8] For example, "God is *love*" (1 Jn. 4:8, 16), and parallel to John 1:1c, "The Word became *flesh*" (Jn. 1:14). Flesh was the quality or nature which the Word "became" at the Incarnation. Similarly, *theos* was the essence which the Word enjoyed "in the beginning." The best translation to pull out the qualitative sense might be, "and the Word was divine."[9] That is to say, "What God was, the Word was."[10] Renowned New Testament Greek grammarian Daniel Wallace concludes:

> The idea of a qualitative θεός [*theos*] here is that the Word had all the attributes and qualities that "the God" (of 1:1b) had. In

anarthrous [without the article]" (*Greek Grammar Beyond the Basics*, 245).

7. Wallace, *Greek Grammar Beyond the Basics*, 43-44, 248, 257.

8. *Ibid.*, 259-260; see also n. 16, citing a study's conclusion that, in John, 94% of predicate nominatives in Colwell's Construction are qualitative.

9. Suggested by Wallace as a modified Moffatt, with the qualification, "… 'divine' is acceptable only if it is a term that can be applied *only* to true deity. However, in modern English, we use it with reference to angels, theologians, even a meal! Thus 'divine' could be misleading in an English translation" (269, emphasis his). Wallace concludes, "Although I believe that θεός [*theos*] in 1:1c is qualitative, I think the simplest and most straightforward translation is, 'and the Word was God.' It may be better to clearly affirm the NT teaching of the deity of Christ and then explain that he is *not* the Father, than to *sound* ambiguous on his deity and explain that he is God but is not the Father" (269, n. 31, emphases his).

10. NEB, qtd. in Wallace, 269. A bad translation, but a helpful teaching paraphrase.

other words, he shared the essence of the Father, though they differed in person. The construction the evangelist chose to express this idea was the most concise way he could have stated that the Word was God and yet was distinct from the Father.[11]

The simple English response to the blasphemy of Jehovah's Witnesses is to read John 1:1 in the context of the entire Gospel.[12] John immediately says in verse 3 that the Word made everything that was made, and without Him, nothing was made that has been made. Therefore, if the Word was made, then He had to make Himself. That is to say, He would have had to exist before He existed, which is logically and physically impossible. The Word must have been uncreated and eternal – not belonging to the category of created beings. This is exactly what John wrote in verse 4, "In Him was life," just like God the Father (cf. 5:26, 11:25, 14:6). In 1:14, John reports he beheld the glory of the Word-become-flesh, full of grace and truth, alluding to the glory of Yahweh in Exodus 34:6-7. John bears true witness that the Word is the God of the Old Testament, Yahweh, the I AM (8:58 and others). Jesus said in John 10:30, "I and the Father are One." Again, everything the Father is, the Son is. As the Council of Nicea righty declared in 325 A.D., They share the same essence.[13] No one can rightly rip 1:1 out of the context of the whole book, which so clearly teaches that Jesus is the Second Member of the Three-in-One God, truly God and truly Man. John 1:18 and 20:28, below, continue to make this explicit.

JOHN 1:18 (AT)
No one has ever seen God; ˏthe˳ One-of-a-kind ˏSon˳, ˏwho is˳ God, the ˏOne˳ being into the bosom of the Father, that ˏOne˳ explained ˏHim˳.

---

11. Wallace, *Greek Grammar Beyond the Basics*, 269, emphases his. Notice that 1:2 repeats "with God" to emphasize the distinction in unity.

12. John Piper, "In The Beginning Was the Word," 21 Sept 2008 (desiringgod.org/sermons/in-the-beginning-was-the-word).

13. *Homoousios* ("same nature"), against the Arian heresy of *homoiousios* ("similar nature"); Grudem, *Systematic Theology*, 244.

The One-of-a-kind[14] Son (1:14) is the One-of-a-kind God in an eternal and intimate relationship with God the Father. Verse 18 closes John's prologue as a chiastic parallel[15] with 1:1:

> A: Word (1:1)
>   B: With God (1:1)
>   C : God (1:1)
>   C$_1$: God (1:18)
>   B$_1$: In the Bosom of the Father (1:18)
> A$_1$: Explained Him (1:18)

As a bookend to John's prologue, 1:18 confirms our interpretation at 1:1 – God the Word is the Self-explanation of the unseen Father (cf. Col. 1:15). Therefore, Jesus could say, "If you have seen Me, you have seen the Father" (14:9). No mere creature could perfectly display the infinite God. But the Word is, uniquely, God!

JOHN 20:28 (AT)
Thomas answered Him, "My Lord and my God!"

We saw in Chapter Six this narrative climax to *The Gospel according to John*. It is worth noting, after the Jehovah's Witnesses' argument over the lack of the definite article in 1:1c, that here Jesus is worshiped as the definite, only God, *ho theos*.[16]

ACTS 20:28 (NASB)
Be on guard for yourselves and for all the flock, among which the Holy Spirit has made you overseers, to shepherd the church of God which He purchased with His own blood.

Since the latter half of the nineteenth century, some have sought an alternate translation to avoid the shocking statement

---

14. See *Part One*, 46, note 6, for the explanation and scholarly support that "only begotten" is a mistranslation of *monogenēs*, which derives from *mono* (only) and *genos* (kind). It also points to ProjectOne28.com/begotten for recent reevaluations.

15. Carson, *John*, 135.

16. Because there is no need, contextually, to distinguish from the Father, as in John 1:1. So Wallace, *Greek Grammar Beyond the Basics*, 268, n. 29.

that God has blood.[17] Obviously, the eternal God is Spirit, and He does not have flesh and blood (Jn. 4:24, Lk. 24:39). But wait; at the fullness of time, God the Son did indeed take on flesh and blood (Jn. 1:14). And He did not cease to be God the Son because of His human nature. How could God cease to be God? How could Jesus have been worshiped while on earth in flesh, if He had become less than God? "Remaining what He was, He became what He was not."[18]

In the One Person of the Lord Jesus Christ are united two natures, divine and human. His human nature is not made super-human (other than human) by its union with His divine nature, or He would not be the substitute for humans, "made like His brothers in every respect... yet without sin" (Heb. 2:17, 4:15). He is true Man. Likewise, His divine nature is not lessened by the union with His human nature, for how could infinite divinity be diminished? He is true God. He is truly the God-Man. Yet He remains One Person, not two persons. Therefore, the death of Jesus Christ was the death of the Second Person of the Trinity, God the

---

17. For example, NET (see the alternative footnotes in ESV and NIV 2011). They take *tou idiou* to be a substantive, rendering instead, "the blood of *His own*," or, "the blood of His own Son." Bowman and Komoszewski make a strong case against it, grammatically: "This reinterpretation of the text is grammatically possible and difficult to disprove absolutely, but it is hardly the most natural reading. As we mentioned, eighteen centuries went by before anyone came up with it. The New Testament nowhere else calls Jesus 'his Own' (*ho idios*), nor was this term ever picked up in the early church as a designation for Jesus. The substantival use of *ho idios* (or any grammatical variation, such as *ton idion*) is, in fact, rare in the New Testament, and in the singular occurs only once – and even then not in reference to a specific person (John 15:19). On the other hand, *ho idios* functions as an adjective following the noun – just as in Acts 20:28 – in several New Testament texts (John 1:41; 5:43; 7:18; Acts 1:25)" (*Putting Jesus in His Place*, 145-146). Stott (*The Cross of Christ*, 154, n. 43) cites early church fathers who referred to "the blood of God" (Ignatius), the "crucified God" (Tertullian), and "the precious and lordly blood of our God" (Gregory of Nazianzus). Modern translations that agree with NASB include ESV, NIV, NKJV, HCSB, LITV, and Wuest.

18. An early church aphorism (Grudem, *Systematic Theology*, 563, not cited). Francis Joseph Hall cited the litany of early church fathers who were fond of this phrase and similar variants: Tertullian, Origen, Athanasius, Hillary, Gregory Nazianzen, Cyril of Alexandria, Theodoret, and Leo the Great (*The Kenotic Theory: Considered with Particular Reference to Its Anglican Forms and Arguments* [New York: Longmans, Green, and Co., 1898], 5-6, n. 2).

Son. As Paul proclaimed to the Ephesian elders in Acts 20:28, the Church was obtained through the infinitely valuable blood of God the Son.

To be clear, God the Son could not die with only a divine nature. God is immortal (1 Tim. 1:17, 6:16). The Son had to become the God-Man to overcome this divine inability to die (Heb. 2:9, 14-17). He experienced suffering and death on the Cross with respect to His human nature. The apostle Peter wrote that He "suffered in the flesh" (1 Pet. 4:1) and was "put to death in the flesh" (3:18). Nevertheless, His human nature was never divorced from His divine Person. As Rob Lister helpfully articulates, "The person of the Son experienced suffering and death *humanly*."[19] More helpful still might be the statement: the Person of *God the Son* experienced suffering and death *humanly*. This alone is Biblical Christianity.

In 1999, the live album *Passion: Better Is One Day* popularized the song, "You Are My King (Amazing Love)." The chorus includes, "Amazing love, how can it be / That You, my King, would die for me?" Many would be surprised to find out that this song by Billy Foote modernized the hymn from Charles Wesley, "And Can It Be," which originally read, "Amazing love! How can it be / That thou, my *God*, should'st die for me?" John Stott defended the original sentiment:

> The reason why both scholarly and simple Christians have felt able to use this kind of language is of course that Scripture permits it. When the apostles wrote of the cross, they often indicated by a tell-tale expression who it was who died there and gave it its efficacy. Thus, he who humbled himself even to death on a cross was none other than he who "being in very nature God" made himself nothing in order to become human and to die (Phil 2:6-8). It was "the Lord of glory" whom the rulers of

---

19. *God Is Impassible and Impassioned*, 274. Lister does not agree with the translation and treatment of Acts 20:28 presented here (see his p. 267), but given his proper Christology, especially seen in this quote, I believe that he could and should. The *divine Person* of the Son was and is the acting subject of His divine *and human* natures.

this age crucified (1 Cor 2:8).... Moreover, the logic of the letter to the Hebrews requires us to say that it is God who died.[20]

To Stott's list, we should add Colossians 1:19-20, where Paul again juxtaposed the blood of Christ's humanity and His divine Person: the peace-making blood of the Cross was shed by the One in whom all the fullness of God was pleased to dwell.

Therefore, the prevailing translation of Acts 20:28 is not only preferable grammatically, but also unobjectionable theologically. Jesus had called "the Assembly of *God*," "*My* Assembly" (Mt. 16:18), because He is God. And with His blood, He bought her. Amazing love, indeed!

> **ROMANS 9:5** (AT)
> whose ,are, the fathers and from whom ,is, the Christ, according to ,the, flesh, the ,One, being God over all, blessed into the ages; amen!

The original Greek manuscripts contained no punctuation, and some have tried to rearrange the punctuation in this sentence so that Christ is not called God.[21] However, the most natural way to understand the participial phrase is that it is functioning like a relative clause: Christ is the One "who is God over all." Paul qualified that the Christ is "from" the unbelieving Israelites only "according to the flesh," which begs for an antithesis.[22] Why did Paul have to qualify it? Because before the Son of God became Jewish flesh to be rejected by His people, He existed and still exists as God over all. Contextually, this magnifies Paul's grief that his

---

20. *The Cross of Christ*, 153. Stott continued to comment on the logic of Heb. 9:15-17, to which I would add that we must also read the exposition of Christ's blood in Hebrews in context of chapter 1, which so forcefully designates Jesus as *theos* (God, see p. 126 below). Cf. the sub-section above, "As God Crucified," on Isa. 53:1, Zech. 12:10, Jn. 19:37 (pp. 110-113). Cf. also the divine redeemer of Titus 2:13-14 on the next page.

21. Douglas J. Moo, *The Epistle to the Romans* (Grand Rapids, MI: Eerdmans, 1996), 566.

22. *Ibid.*, 567. Murray J. Harris, "If there was no sense in which ὁ Χριστός ["the Christ"] was not purely of Jewish stock, Paul would have concluded his statement simply with Χριστός. As it is, τὸ κατὰ σάρκα ["according to the flesh"] suggests there is an aspect of Christ's person to which the category of human descent is inapplicable" (*Prepositions*

"kinsmen according to the flesh" were accursed away from Christ
– not merely a human Messiah, but God Himself, who deserves the
"worship" entrusted to their forefathers (9:2-4). Paul, representing
true Israelites, blessed Jesus Christ as God, exalted with sovereign
authority over all things.

> ### TITUS 2:13-14 (AT)
> …waiting for the happy hope and epiphany of, the
> glory of, our great God and Savior Jesus Christ, [14]who
> gave Himself for us, in order that He may redeem us
> for Himself, from all lawlessness and that, He may
> cleanse for, Himself a, people for His own possession,
> zealous for, good works.

> ### 2 PETER 1:1
> … To those who have obtained a faith of equal
> standing with ours by the righteousness of our God
> and Savior Jesus Christ….

The Greek behind "our God and Savior" in these two
passages fits Sharp's Rule: in an article-substantive-and-substantive
construction in which both substantives are singular, personal, and
not proper names, both substantives refer to the same person.[23]
There are no exceptions to this rule in the New Testament.[24]
Christopher Wordsworth of Trinity College in Cambridge
exhaustively investigated 1,000 years of Greek Christian literature
from the early church, finding no single exception to Sharp's Rule.[25]

---

and Theology in the Greek New Testament: An Essential Reference Resource for Exegesis
[Grand Rapids, MI: Zondervan, 2012], 148).

23. Wallace, *Greek Grammar Beyond the Basics*, 271-272. It is important to grasp Wallace's
note: "A *proper* noun is defined as a noun which cannot be 'pluralized' – thus it does
not include titles. A person's name, therefore, is proper and consequently does not fit
the rule. But θεός [*theos*, "God"] is not proper because it can be pluralized – thus,
when θεός is in a TSKS construction in which both nouns are singular and personal,
it fits Sharp's rule. Since θεοί [*theoi*, "gods"] is possible (cf. John 10:34), θεός is not
a proper name" (272, n. 42, emphasis his, cf. his example from Jn. 20:17 on p. 274).
This also supports our foundational contention that "God" and "Lord" are titles, not
the personal Name of Yahweh.

24. *Ibid.*, 273, see also n. 50.

25. *Ibid.*, 277, n. 62.

Therefore, in these verses, we can be certain that Jesus Christ is both God and Savior. Furthermore, "… in the first century, the formula 'God and Savior' was a common religious expression used by both Palestinian and Diaspora Jews in reference to Yahweh…."[26] Jesus is Yahweh, the one true God and Savior.

HEBREWS 1:8-12

But of the Son he says,
 "Your throne, O God, is forever and ever,
        the scepter of uprightness is the scepter of your kingdom.
[9]You have loved righteousness and hated wickedness;
therefore God, your God, has anointed you
        with the oil of gladness beyond your companions."

[10]And,

 "You, Lord, laid the foundation of the earth in the beginning,
        and the heavens are the work of your hands;
[11]they will perish, but you remain;
        they will all wear out like a garment,
[12]like a robe you will roll them up,
        like a garment they will be changed.
But you are the same,
        and your years will have no end."

We studied verses 8-9 in Chapter Five, quoting the prophecy in Psalm 45:6-7 that the Messiah would be God in relationship with God. Here we see the context continued to apply the worship of Yahweh in Psalm 102:25-27 to Jesus, the eternal, unchanging Creator.

1 JOHN 5:20 (AT)

But we know that the Son ‚of‚ God has come and has given ‚to‚ us ‚a‚ mind in order that we may know the true ‚One‚‚ and we are in the true ‚One‚‚ in His Son, Jesus Christ. *This ‚One‚ is the true God and eternal life.*

---

26. Stephen Wellum, "The Deity of Christ in the Apostolic Witness," in *The Deity of Christ*, 146; cf. n. 118, "In addition, the phrase 'God and Savior' was a common formula in the Greco-Roman world, and it regularly refers to one deity in such formulas. There is no reason to think that Paul [or Peter] departs from this standard usage."

Some translations unhelpfully render, "He is the true God…," instead of, "This One,…." The Greek *houtos* ("this") is the near demonstrative, which, most simply, points emphatically to the nearest antecedent, in this case, "Jesus Christ."[27] Furthermore, *houtos* verges on a technical theological term for John, who favors using it to point emphatically to Jesus. Köstenberger summarizes the grammatical considerations well:

> …as Daniel Wallace points out, of the approximately seventy instances in John's Gospel and letters in which *houtos* has a personal referent, at least two-thirds refer to the Son, while not a single one refers to the Father.[28]

That "This One" refers to Jesus is the clearest reading of the Greek, both grammatically and theologically. Just as Jesus had taught John, "I AM the way and the truth and life," John faithfully reported that Jesus Christ is "the true God and eternal life."[29] And just as John climaxed his Gospel with Thomas' confession of Jesus as God (20:28), John also culminated his Epistle with his own confession of Jesus as God.[30]

Some might think it odd that the New Testament only calls Jesus *theos* nine times. First, let us admit how amazing it is that it says it at all! We should also realize that it is rare because *theos* typically designated God *the Father*, and the writers took care not to confuse the distinct Members of the Trinity. But we must also

---

27. See Wallace, *Greek Grammar Beyond the Basics*, 325-327. Some interpret this to be declaring that God the Father is the true God, since He is called "the true One" earlier in the verse, as well as "God" in v. 19 (cf. also Jn. 17:3, connecting eternal life to knowing the only true God, the Father). Comfort and Hawley ask, "But what is the point of saying this? Of course, God is the true God. John would not have needed to say this. Rather, he was affirming Jesus' deity, as he had earlier affirmed Jesus' humanity (4:1-6)" (Philip W. Comfort & Wendell C. Hawley, *1-3 John* [Carol Stream, IL: Tyndale House, 2007], 373).

28. Andreas J. Köstenberger, "The Deity of Christ in John's Letters and the Book of Revelation," in *The Deity of Christ*, 155.

29. Cf. Jn. 14:6, cf. 1:4, 5:26. So also Wallace, *Greek Grammar Beyond the Basics*, 327.

30. Köstenberger, "The Deity of Christ in John's Letters and the Book of Revelation," in *The Deity of Christ*, 155-156, n. 11.

keep in mind that *theos* is not the only way to honor Jesus as divine, and the New Testament is replete with other divine appellations for Jesus.

JESUS AS *THEOS* (GOD)	
JOHN 1:1	"and the Word was God"
JOHN 1:18	"the One-of-a-kind God... being into the bosom of the Father"
JOHN 20:28	"My Lord and my God!"
ACTS 20:28	"the church of God... obtained through His own blood"
ROMANS 9:5	"Christ, the One being God over all, blessed into the ages"
TITUS 2:13-14	"our great God and Savior Jesus Christ"
2 PETER 1:1	"our God and Savior Jesus Christ"
HEBREWS 1:8	"Your throne, O God, is forever and ever"
1 JOHN 5:20	"This One is the true God and eternal life"

AS *KURIOS* (YAHWEH)

In New Testament Greek, *kurios* ("lord") is used in four senses: polite address (like our "sir"), owner, master, and religiously as the substitute for *YHWH*.[31] We noted earlier that the earliest extant manuscripts of the *Greek* Old Testament wrote the Tetragram in *Hebrew* script. Most, however, came to replace it with *kurios*, matching the practice of pronouncing "Adonai" instead of "Yahweh." John Frame notes that the New Testament writers "also use *kyrios*, as in the Old Testament, to refer to God the Father, which provides further confirmation that they regarded the term as a divine title."[32] The Gospels also frame the coming of Christ as the coming of "the Lord," Yahweh, such that even the polite address, "Sir" (*kurios*), by unbelievers becomes ironic. Readers are encouraged to think, "If they only knew how true that title is...."

---

31. Gathercole, *The Preexistent Son*, 243.

Mark 1:1-3, "The beginning of the gospel of Jesus Christ, *the Son of God*. As it is written in the prophet Isaiah... Prepare the way of *the Lord*." In our English New Testaments, "Lord" always appears in regular font, not small caps, as it frequently does in the Old. The reason is, whereas the Old Testament originally contained the Hebrew *YHWH*, the New Testament originally contained the Greek *kurios*, even when quoting translations of the Old Testament. Therefore, students of the New Testament must be careful to look back to the Old Testament reference to see if "LORD" or "GOD" signifies *YHWH* or if "Lord" translates *Adonai/Kurios*. Case in point, Mark 1:3 appears with regular case "Lord." But flipping back to the quoted passage, Isaiah 40:3, we find small caps, "LORD," alerting us to the original *YHWH*. John the Baptist prepared the way for the LORD, Jesus. Therefore, the earliest Gospel in its earliest verses introduces Jesus as Yahweh in one of the clearest ways possible.

Acts 2:21, 36. At Pentecost, Peter quoted the fulfillment of Joel 2:32: "everyone who calls upon the Name of the Lord [Yahweh] shall be saved" (Acts 2:21). Then Peter closed with, "Let all the house of Israel therefore know for certain that God has made him both Lord and Christ, this Jesus whom you crucified" (2:36). Peter identified Jesus as the Yahweh of Joel 2:32. He has always been Yahweh the Son, and the Father also appointed Him to be the Christ, crucified, resurrected, reigning, and saving. The book of Acts continues to designate Jesus as Lord frequently, for example, Peter's proclamation in 10:36 that He is "Lord of all," Yahweh, sovereign over all His creation (cf. Rom. 10:12 below).

Romans 10:9-13. In one of the most famous passages in Romans, part of "the Roman road" in evangelism, Paul asserts, "Because if you confess with your mouth Jesus to be, Lord[33] and believe in your heart that God raised Him from the dead, you will

---

32. *The Doctrine of God*, 653, n. 16, citing Matt. 1:20; 9:38; 11:25; Acts 17:24; Rev. 4:11.

33. The Greek structure is a double accusative (cf. 2 Cor. 4:5), not a predicate nominative as it is in Phil. 2:9-11 and 1 Cor. 12:3, "Jesus is Lord."

be saved" (10:9, AT). In what immediately follows, Paul leaves no doubt which of the four senses of *kurios* he means: there is one Lord of all (10:12, clearly Yahweh), and, "everyone who calls upon the Name of the Lord will be saved" (10:13, quoting Joel 2:32). Paul explicitly connects "Jesus as Lord" in 10:9 with Yahweh of Joel 2:32. *We must believe that Jesus is Yahweh the Son – crucified, raised, and reigning – in order to be saved!*

Philippians 2:6-11. In Philippians 2:6, Paul says that, before the incarnation, Jesus was *"existing in the nature of God... equal with God"* (AT). Jesus is God the Son, sharing the same essence as God the Father and Spirit. Then He humbled Himself to take on the "nature of a bondservant," the "likeness of men" (2:7).[34] God the Son became the God-Man, in order to die on the Cross (2:8).

> Therefore God has highly exalted him and bestowed on him the name that is above every name, [10]so that at the name of Jesus every knee should bow, in heaven and on earth and under the earth, [11]and every tongue confess that Jesus Christ is *Lord*, to the glory of God the Father (2:9-11).

Through the God-Man's humble, obedient death, God has raised Him, seated Him on His throne, and bestowed upon Him the Name above every Name. What Name is that? Jesus? The emphasis of passage lands on "Lord," standing in for the matchless Name: Yahweh. The confirmation of Paul's meaning comes with recognition of the Old Testament allusion:

> ISAIAH 45:21-25 (AT)
> …Who told this long ago?
>   Who declared it of old?
> Was it not I, Yahweh?
>   And there is no other god besides Me,
> a righteous God and a Savior;
>   there is none besides Me.
>
> [22]"Turn to Me and be saved,
>   all the ends of the earth!
>   Because I am God, and there is no other.

²³By myself I have sworn;
> from My mouth has gone out in righteousness
> a word that will not return:
'To Me every knee will bow,
> every tongue will swear allegiance.'
²⁴Only in Yahweh, it will be said of Me,
> are righteousness and strength;
to Him will come and be ashamed
> all who were incensed against Him.
²⁵In Yahweh all the seed of Israel
> will be declared righteous and will exult.

Yahweh had said that the bowing and confessing would be done "to Me" (Isa. 45:23). Strikingly, Paul, a Hebrew of Hebrews, took a passage that unequivocally declares there is only One God and Savior, Yahweh, and he applied it to Jesus, "unto the glory of God the Father" – not two gods, but distinct Persons inseparably united in One God. *At the final judgment, every human will say, likely in their own languages with this common understanding, "Jesus Christ is Yahweh!"* Some will begrudgingly admit it with shame and incense (Isa. 45:24) before being condemned to everlasting punishment. We must bid "the ends of the earth" (45:22) to repent, before it is too late, and join the host of true Israel, comprised of every tribe and tongue who "exult" in this statement of faith (45:25).

1 Corinthians 1:30 and 6:11. We saw above, in Isaiah 45:25, that God promised the seed of Israel would be declared righteous in the Name of Yahweh. Because Jesus is Yahweh, Paul wrote, "you were declared righteous in the Name of the *Lord* Jesus Christ" (1 Cor. 6:11, AT). Earlier, he wrote that Christ Jesus became our righteousness (1:30). This fulfilled the prophecy that, in the days of salvation, the Davidic Messiah would be called *Yahweh-tsidkenu*, "Yahweh-Our-Righteousness" (Jer. 23:5-6, 33:16). Christ is "*the* Righteous One" (1 Jn. 2:1, cf. Isa. 53:11), and His righteousness, grace-gifted to us, is the righteousness of Yahweh.

---

34. See Grudem's fine refutation of the "kenosis theory" (*Systematic Theology*, 549-552).

Romans 9:33 and 1 Peter 2:8, 3:15. In Romans 9:33, Paul crafted a composite quotation from Isaiah 28:16 about the Messiah and from Isaiah 8:14 about Yahweh. Yahweh warned Isaiah not to fear conspiratorial threats of the Syrians and Israelites as the rest of Judah did (8:11-12). The dreadful prospect of forsaking Yahweh should outweigh the fear of snubbing any human super-powers:

> But Yahweh of hosts, *him you shall honor as holy.* Let him be your fear, and let him be your dread. [14]And he will become a sanctuary and *a stone of offense and a rock of stumbling* to both houses of Israel, a trap and a snare to the inhabitants of Jerusalem. [15]And many shall stumble on it. They shall fall and be broken; they shall be snared and taken (8:13-15).

Yahweh promised to become a stone in the way of all Israelites, who will not be able to evade Him (8:14). Then He promised the Messiah would be a stone (28:16). Paul, in his composite quotation, taught that both passages were fulfilled in the God-Man: Jesus is the Yahweh of Isaiah 8:14 and the Messiah of 28:16. Peter also applied the phrase in Isaiah 8:13 about regarding Yahweh as holy to "Christ the *Lord*" (1 Pet. 3:15).

Jesus had started the tradition of referring to Him as this stone. He first quoted Psalm 118:22-23 about the Messiah as the stone rejected by the builders but chosen by Yahweh (Mt. 21:42). Then He alluded to unbelievers falling over and being broken on Him as the Yahweh of Isaiah 8:14 (Mt. 21:44a). And finally, He added an allusion to the divinely cut stone of Daniel 2, crushing His opponents (Mt. 21:44b). Peter also strung together these three prophetic passages (1 Pet. 2:4-8). Jesus is not only a human Messiah; He is Yahweh become flesh, the God-Man.

1 Peter 2:2-3. Immediately before Peter applied Isaiah 8:14 to Jesus, he exhorted the believers to "yearn for the rational, pure milk, in order that, by it, you may grow into salvation, if you tasted that the Lord is good."[35] Peter alluded to Psalm 34:8, "Taste and see that the LORD is good." Therefore, tasting Jesus is tasting Yahweh. Delight yourself in Him!

Ephesians 4:8-10. Paul quoted Psalm 68:18 about the victory of Yahweh at the Exodus, explaining it was ultimately fulfilled in the incarnation, resurrected ascension, and gift-giving of Christ. In both the foreshadow and the substance, Jesus has done what only Yahweh can do. If G. V. Smith is correct that the receiving and giving of gifts in Psalm 68 itself alluded to Yahweh's taking and giving the Levites as a gift to the Israelites (Num. 8:6, 14; 18:6), then Paul introduces this quotation as the historical foreshadow to his next verses: Christ gives apostles, prophets, evangelists, shepherds, and teachers as gifts to the New Covenant Church (Eph. 4:11-12).[36] This would lengthen and strengthen the already obvious teaching that Jesus acts as Yahweh.

1 Corinthians 1:31, 2:8; Philippians 3:3. Paul paraphrased Jeremiah 9:24 as, "Let the one who boasts, boast in the Lord" (1 Cor. 1:31). In Jeremiah the Name is Yahweh. In Paul's context, one might lean to interpreting that God the Father is the referent of *kurios* (vv. 18-30). In 2:8, though, Jesus is "the [*kurios*] Lord of glory."[37] And in Philippians 3:3, Paul defines the true circumcision as those who "boast in Christ Jesus" (AT, with the same verbal root as 1 Cor. 1:31). Therefore, Jesus is the Yahweh of Jeremiah 9, worthy of our exultation.

The Day of Yahweh. One of the major themes in the Prophets is "the day of Yahweh," when He will come to judge His enemies and save His people.[38] Repeatedly in the New Testament, "the day

---

35. First Peter 2:2-3 (AT). That Peter refers to Jesus as "Lord" here becomes clear from the pronouns following in verse 4.

36. For consideration, see Peter T. O'Brien, *The Letter to the Ephesians,* The Pillar New Testament Commentary (Grand Rapids, MI: Eerdmans, 1999), 292-293.

37. "Paul uses *kurios* exclusively to refer to Christ" (Gordon D. Fee, *Pauline Christology: An Exegetical-Theology Study* [Peabody, MA: Hendrickson, 2007], 525, qtd. in Peterson, "Toward a Systematic Theology of the Deity of Christ," in *The Deity of Christ,* 205).

38. E.g., Isa. 13:6, 9, 58:13; Jer. 46:10, Ezek. 13:5, 30:3; Joel 1:15, 2:1, 11, 31, 3:14, Am.

of the Lord" is "the day of our Lord Jesus Christ" and "the coming of our Lord Jesus Christ" and "the day of Jesus Christ" and "the day of Christ."[39] This provides another unmistakable identification of Jesus as Yahweh. The ancient promises that Yahweh will come for salvation through judgment both have been fulfilled in Jesus' first coming and will be consummated in His second coming. Let all the earth revere Him!

2 Thessalonians 1:7-9. Paul comforted the afflicted Thessalonians with the gospel promise that "the Lord Jesus" will be "revealed from heaven with his mighty angels" – because He is God of the angels – "in flaming fire, inflicting vengeance on those who do not know God and on those who do not obey the gospel of our Lord Jesus" (vv. 7-8). The Greek for "in flaming fire" and "inflicting vengeance" both appear in Isaiah 66:15 (LXX) of Yahweh's coming.[40] Paul continued, "They will suffer the punishment of eternal destruction, away from the presence of the Lord and from the glory of his might" (1:9). The Greek for "away from the presence [lit., face] of the Lord" and "from the glory of His might" echoes the refrain in Isaiah 2:10, 19, and 21 regarding the day of Yahweh (cf. 2:12).[41] Again in Paul's rich

SELECT PASSAGES OF JESUS AS *KURIOS* (YAHWEH)	
MK. 1:1-3	EPH. 4:8-10
ACTS 2:21, 36	PHIL. 2:9-11
ROM. 9:33	2 THESS. 1:7-9
10:9-13	1 PET. 2:3
1 COR. 1:8	2:8
1:30	3:15
1:31	REV. 17:14
2:8	19:16
6:11	

5:20, Ob. 1:15, Zeph. 1:7, 8, 14; Mal. 4:5.

39. 1 Cor. 1:8; 2 Cor. 1:14; 2 Thess. 2:1-2; Phil. 1:6, 10, 2:16; cf. also "the day of the Lord" in 1 Cor. 5:5, in which context Jesus is the Lord with power to judge (v. 4); cf. also "the day of the Lord" in 1 Thess. 5:2, in which context Jesus is the coming Lord (1:1, 2:19, 4:15-17, 5:9, 23). As a matter of fact, "Paul uses *kurios* exclusively to refer to Christ" (Fee, see n. 37 above). Cf. also "the day of the Lord" in 2 Pet. 3:10, in which context Jesus is the Lord (3:16).

40. See Jeffrey A. D. Weima, *CNTUOT*, 884, for the difficulties with the textual criticism and identification of the allusion. Weima concludes the allusion is to Isa. 66:15.

41. *Ibid.*, 885.

prose, Jesus is Yahweh the Son, a consuming fire, whose holiness rightly responds to unrepentant sinners with vengeance. The Church will be saved and granted relief from persecution when Yahweh-in-flesh returns to cast the disbelieving into hell. Let all the earth obey His gospel before that day!

Revelation 17:14 and 19:16. In John's vision of the returning Jesus, "On his robe and on his thigh he has a name written, King of kings and Lord of lords" (Rev. 19:16, cf. 17:14). The titles employ a Hebraism, such as "Holy of Holies," which means "the Holiest Holy" or "the Most Holy Place." The "heaven of heavens" is the heavenliest heaven, "the highest heaven."[42] Likewise, Jesus is the kingliest King and the lordliest Lord, the greatest, the preeminent One. The title "Lord of lords" was first ascribed to Yahweh in Deuteronomy 10:17, "For Yahweh your God is God of gods and Lord of lords, the great, the mighty, the awesome God...."[43] Jesus is He! And Jesus' supreme Godhood is the guarantee[44] of His victory in the final war.

OTHER ASCRIPTIONS OF GODHOOD TO JESUS

Seated on God's Throne. Perhaps the New Testament writers' favorite psalm is Psalm 110, written by David, which begins: "Yahweh said to my Lord, 'Sit at my right hand until I make your enemies your footstool'" (v. 1). The apostolic preachers and writers quoted and alluded to it frequently to point to Jesus' exalted position where He reigns over all things in heaven and on earth.[45] Jesus

---

42. E.g., Ex. 26:33, Neh. 9:6

43. Cf. Ps. 136:3, Dn. 2:47; 1 Tim. 6:15. See G. K. Beale, *The Book of Revelation,* NIGCT (Grand Rapids, MI: Eerdmans, 1999), 881, for the parallel with Dan. 4:37 (LXX), "because he himself is God of gods and Lord of lords and King of kings." He also notes, "Almost the same title occurs... for God in Dan. 2:47," as well as pointing out the other allusions to Daniel in the immediate context of Rev. 17. Cf. Grant R. Osborne, *Revelation,* BECNT (Grand Rapids, MI: Baker Academic, 2002), 623.

44. Note the "for" (or "because") in Rev. 17:14.

45. Carson calls it "the most frequently quoted OT chapter in the NT" (*Matthew,* 467). Also Peter T. O'Brien, *The Letter to the Hebrews,* PNTC (Grand Rapids, MI: Eerdmans, 2010), 78. (Factor in that the NT also quotes the Melchizedek promise of 110:4.)

had first applied this verse to Himself to confound the Pharisees that they must conceive of the Christ as greater than simply a human son of David (Mt. 22:41-46).[46] Then He employed it as part of His good confession which ensured the Sanhedrin would condemn Him for blasphemy (Mt. 26:64). A. B. Ehrlich draws out the correct implication, which elicited their violent reaction: "From the Old Testament point of view it was wholly unthinkable, even in metaphor, to describe a mortal as seated on Yahweh's right hand."[47] Indeed, Jesus must be more than a mere mortal. He shares the essence and sovereignty of God the Father. Having finished the work of redemption, He will sit enthroned until the Father sends Him again to rid the planet of His enemies (Ps. 110:5-7; 1 Cor. 15:24-28).

Aramaic "Lord." At the close of his letter, Paul transliterated an Aramaic phrase for his Greek audience. (Aramaic was the common language for Jews in Palestine during Jesus' time. Some portions of the Old Testament had been written in Aramaic.[48]) That Paul would use an Aramaic phrase, without explanation, in a letter to Greek-speaking Gentiles far away from Palestine, shows that this phrase must have been popular in the early church and well-known even to the Corinthians. Paul wrote: *"Maranatha!"* (1 Cor. 16:22). The original Greek manuscripts did not contain any spaces between words, and the two possibilities for breaking up the phrase are *marana tha* or *maran atha*. The first is the most popular understanding today, as a petition: "Our Lord, come!" However, the second division is how the Middle Eastern church (Jesus'

---

46. Carson, "If Messiah is not David's son, *whose son is he?* The solution is given by the prologue to Matthew (chs. 1-2) and by the voice of God himself (3:17; 17:5): Jesus is the Son of God.... What Jesus does is synthesize the concept of a human Messiah in David's line with the concept of a divine Messiah who transcends human limitations (e.g., Ps 45:6-7; Isa 9:6; Jer 23:5-6; 33:15-16; Zech 12:10 [MT]; 13:7 [NASB])..." (*Matthew*, 468, emphasis his).

47. Qtd. in Bruce K. Waltke, *Old Testament Theology* (Grand Rapids, MI: Zondervan, 2007), 895, qtd. in Ortlund, "The Deity of Christ and the Old Testament," in *The Deity of Christ*, 48.

48. Gen. 31:47, Ezra 4:8–6:18, 7:12-26, Jer. 10:11, Dan. 2:4–7:28, and on Jesus' lips: Mk.

region) understood it for at least its first sixteen hundred years, as a confession: "Our Lord has come!"[49] Either way, the earliest Jewish Christians – and even Greek Christians – were calling Jesus their *Marē*, "Lord," the One true God of Aramaic passages like Daniel 2:47 and 5:23!

The Lord's Supper. Jesus redefined the elements of the Jewish Passover meal to point to Himself and the New Exodus He accomplished through His body and blood (Lk. 22:7-22). Hence, it become known as "the Lord's Supper," reoriented from honoring Yahweh to honoring Jesus, who must then be viewed as Yahweh the Son in flesh. In Paul's admonition in 1 Corinthians 10:14-22, he contrasts the Lord's Supper with pagan sacrifices offered "to demons and not *to God*" (v. 20). Gordon Fee rightly concludes, "Thus Paul's clear setting out of the Lord's Table as the Christian alternative to these pagan meals assumes that Christ is the Christian deity who is honored at his meal."[50] Each time we participate in the broken bread and the cup of blessing, may our hearts be filled with more than gratefulness to a mere man, but worshipful adoration of the God-Man.

Creator and Sovereign Sustainer. Colossians 1 contains a hymn to Jesus as the One who stands outside of created time as the Giver, Governor, and Goal of all things. "All things were created [by Him, v. 15, and] through Him and for Him" (v. 16), and, " He is before all things, and in Him all things hold together" (v. 17). Scientists call it gravity; we call Him the beloved Son of God (v. 13). The grand doctrine in the Hebrew Scriptures of the Providence of God is thus invested in Jesus. "Because in Him all the fullness was pleased to dwell" (1:19, AT), and, "Because in Him all the fullness

---

5:41, 7:34, Mt. 27:46 (also, *Golgotha* is an Aramaic name, Mk. 15:22).

49. Kenneth E. Bailey, *Paul Through Mediterranean Eyes: Cultural Studies in 1 Corinthians* (Downers Grove, IL: IVP Academic, 2011), 495-497, qtd. in Trevin Wax, "The Meaning of 'Maranatha,'" 2 Feb 2012 (thegospelcoalition.org/blogs/trevinwax/2012/02/02/the-meaning-of-maranatha/).

50. *Pauline Christology*, 492, qtd. in Peterson, "Toward a Systematic Theology of the Deity of Christ," in *The Deity of Christ*, 203.

of, Godhood dwells bodily" (2:9, AT). Just as Isaiah 9 prophesied, the Father, Son, and Holy Spirit all indwell the Christ because the Triune God is inseparable.[51] He "is the image of, the unseen God" (1:15, AT, cf. 2 Cor. 4:4), and as such, He deserves to receive what is His – all things.

The author of Hebrews honors the Son as the One "through whom [God the Father] made the ages, who is the, radiance of, His glory and the, exact representation of, His Being..." (1:2-3, AT). Donald Hagner wrote: "for the Son to be the kind of direct, authentic, and compelling expression of the Father described in these phrases... he must participate somehow in the being of God itself, that is, he must himself be deity to accomplish the wonderful mission described here."[52] Peter O'Brien concludes: "he is able to be God's historical self-revelation because he is identified with Yahweh himself."[53] As we discovered in *Part One*, God's glory does not only shine forth abstractly; God's glory is so infinitely perfect that it manifests as a Person, the Son, identical to the Father.[54] Donald Macleod eloquently says this is "not a different glory from the Father's but the same glory in another form. The Father is the glory hidden; the Son is the glory revealed."[55]

The praise of Hebrews 1 continues: "...carrying all things by, the word of, His power..." (v. 3, AT). Every moment, everything is here because the Son of God is saying, "Be there!" His word is not merely propping up all things, like Atlas; His word is, literally, "carrying" all things to their appointed destination.[56] "What is

---

51. See pp. 84-85, esp. notes 41-42 on p. 85; see also, Grudem, *Systematic Theology*, 252.

52. D. A. Hagner, *Encountering the Book of Hebrews: An Exposition* (Grand Rapids, MI: Baker, 2002), 24, qtd. in O'Brien, *Hebrews*, 56.

53. *Hebrews*, 56.

54. *Part One*, 45-51, 55-56, esp. 47 (free at ProjectOne28.com/glory).

55. *The Person of Christ* (Downers Grove, IL: InterVarsity, 1998), 80, qtd. in Wellum, "The Deity of Christ in the Apostolic Witness," in *The Deity of Christ*, 137, n. 93.

56. Frame, *The Doctrine of God*, 276. Also, O'Brien, *Hebrews*, 56-57 (citing also Bruce, Lane, and Grässer). Grudem explains: "The Greek word [typically] translated 'upholding' is *pherō*, 'carry, bear.' This is commonly used in the New Testament for

here being ascribed to the Son is the providential government of the universe, which is the function of God himself."[57] The Son is the sovereign Yahweh, steering what He is sustaining – all things.

Doxologies. "Doxologies, by their very nature, were addressed to the one God who alone is worthy of eternal glory and worship."[58] Therefore, it is so significant that Jesus is the object of numerous doxologies in Scripture. We noted Romans 9:5 above, that Christ is "God over all, blessed into the ages, amen!" In 2 Timothy 4:18, Paul could not help but praise, "To Him be, the glory into the ages of, the ages; amen!" (AT). Peter closed his second letter on this worshipful note: "But be growing in the, grace and knowledge of, our Lord and Savior Jesus Christ. To Him be, the glory both now and into the, day of, eternity" (2 Pet. 3:18, AT).

Notice the way Jude includes Jesus as Lord in his doxology of the Father: "…to the, only God, our Savior, through Jesus Christ our Lord be, glory, majesty, might, and authority before every age and now and into all the ages; amen!" (v. 25, AT). God the Father possessed and manifested these attributes *through Jesus Christ* before every age, that is, before time began. That can be true only if Jesus preexisted in the eternal past as God the Son, the radiance of His glory![59]

The prologue to Revelation joins the chorus: "To, the One who, is loving us and released us from our sins by His blood, … to, Him be, the glory and the might into the ages of, the ages; amen!"

---

carrying something from one place to another… [e.g., Lk. 5:18, Jn. 2:8; 2 Tim. 4:13]. It does not mean simply 'sustain,' but has the sense of active, purposeful control over the thing being carried from one place to another" (*Systematic Theology*, 316). Frame describes Heb. 1:3 as "a dynamic image of him carrying the world from one point to another through time. There is a destination, and Christ's purpose is to bring the world process to that goal, that conclusion" (276).

57. Montefiore, 35, cited in D. J. Ebert, "Wisdom in New Testament Christology, with Special Reference to Hebrews 1:1-4" (unpub. Ph.D. thesis, Trinity Evangelical Divinity School, 1998), 89, qtd. in O'Brien, *Hebrews*, 57.

58. Köstenberger, "The Deity of Christ in John's Letters and the Book of Revelation," in *The Deity of Christ*, 163.

59. Harris, *Prepositions and Theology in the Greek New Testament*, 97. Cf. Jude 5 *(see p. 70)*.

(1:5-6, AT). God as Spirit has no blood, but a man as man cannot receive glory due only to God; worshiping One who ransomed us by His blood only makes sense if He is the God-Man.

Hymns. Because of their structure in the original Greek, Colossians 1:15-20 and Philippians 2:6-8 are considered hymns, sung *to Jesus* by the early Church.[60] Paul encouraged this in Ephesians 5:18-19, explaining that one result of "being filled by, the Spirit" is "singing and psalming ,with, your heart ,to, the Lord" (AT). The Lord is identified in the very next clause as "Jesus Christ" (v. 20). Therefore, the frequent Old Testament command, "Sing to Yahweh,"[61] was applied to the LORD Jesus Christ. When Athanasius was faithfully defending the Godhood of Christ in the fourth century against the Arian heresy, one of his main points was that the Church rightly worshiped Jesus, which would be idolatry, except that He truly is God.[62]

So much more evidence could be presented, but this summary of Paul's writings from David Wells drives home the point well:

> Consequently, Paul moves easily into a complete linguistic identification of Christ with Yahweh. If Yahweh is our sanctifier (Ex. 31:13), is omnipresent (Ps. 139:7-10), is our peace (Judg. 6:24), is our righteousness (Jer. 23:6), is our victory (Ex. 17:8-16), and is our healer (Ex. 15:26), then so is Christ all of these things (1 Cor. 1:30; Col. 1:27; Eph. 2:14). If the gospel is God's (1 Thess. 2:2, 6-9; Gal. 3:8), then that same gospel is also Christ's (1 Thess. 3:2; Gal. 1:7). If the church is God's (Gal. 1:13; 1 Cor. 15:9), then that same church is also Christ's (Rom. 16:16). God's Kingdom (1 Thess. 2:12) is Christ's (Eph. 5:5); God's love (Eph. 1:3-5) is Christ's (Rom. 8:35); God's Word (Col. 1:25; 1 Thess. 2:13) is Christ's (1 Thess. 1:8; 4:15); God's Spirit (1 Thess. 4:8) is Christ's (Phil. 1:19); God's peace (Gal.

---

60. See Wallace, *Greek Grammar Beyond the Basics*, 340-341 (cf. n. 67).

61. E.g., Ex. 15:21; 1 Chron. 16:23; 2 Chron. 20:21, Ps. 95:1, 96:1, 2, 98:1, 147:7, 149:1, Isa. 42:10 (cf. Rev. 5:9), Jer. 20:13; *Putting Jesus in His Place*, 55.

62. Alister E. McGrath, *Historical Theology: An Introduction to the History of Christian Thought*, Second Ed. (West Sussex, UK: Wiley-Blackwell, 2013), 45; Frame, *The*

5:22; Phil. 4:9) is Christ's (Col. 3:15; cf Col. 1:2; Phil. 1:2; 4:7); God's 'Day' of judgment (Isa. 13:6) is Christ's 'Day' of judgment (Phil. 1:6, 10; 2:16; 1 Cor. 1:8); God's grace (Eph. 2:8, 9; Col. 1:6; Gal. 1:15) is Christ's grace (1 Thess. 5:28; Gal. 1:6; 6:18); God's salvation (Col. 1:13) is Christ's salvation (1 Thess. 1:10); and God's will (Eph. 1:11; 1 Thess. 4:3; Gal. 1:4) is Christ's will (Eph. 5:17; cf. 1 Thess. 5:18). So it is no surprise to hear Paul say that he is both God's slave (Rom. 1:9) and Christ's (Rom. 1:1; Gal. 1:10), that he lives for that glory which is both God's (Rom. 5:2; Gal. 1:24) and Christ's (2 Cor. 8:19, 23; cf. 2 Cor. 4:6), that his faith is in God (1 Thess. 1:8, 9; Rom. 4:1-5) and in Christ Jesus (Gal. 3:22), and that to know God, which is salvation (Gal. 4:8; 1 Thess. 4:5), is to know Christ (2 Cor. 4:6).[63]

As God in Revelation

The Ancient of Days. The Bible's final book leaves no doubt that Jesus is God the Son. In the commissioning vision, the apostle John saw Jesus as "one *like* a son of man" (Rev. 1:13), the *divine* figure foreseen in Daniel 7:13-14. The visual description of Him in Revelation 1 matches point for point the divine "Man" who appeared in Daniel 10 (see the chart on p. 78). In the rich imagery of Jesus' eternal glory, the most noteworthy item, for our purposes here, comes from verse 14: "The hairs of his head were white, like white wool, like snow." This corresponds to the description in Daniel 7, not of the Son of Man, but of the Ancient of Days! "As I looked, thrones were placed, and the Ancient of Days took his seat; his clothing was white as snow, and the hair of his head like pure wool…" (Dan. 7:9). Jesus is the Son of Man who is the image of the eternal God. The symbol of white hair communicates that He is worthy to be revered as the end-times Judge,[64] white like snow because He is pure and holy.[65]

Doctrine of God, 733. Interestingly, Pliny the Younger, the pagan Roman governor of Pontus-Bithynia (c. 111-13 A.D.), wrote in a letter to Emperor Trajan about his persecution of Christians, who "had been accustomed to meet before daybreak and to recite a hymn antiphonally to Christ, as to a god" (qtd. in *How God Became Jesus*, 169).

63. *The Person of Christ*, 64-65, to which I was pointed by the partial quotation in Peterson,

"And His voice is like the voice of many waters" (1:15, AT). In Ezekiel 1:24 the sound of many waters is paralleled with the sound of the Almighty (cf. 43:2). This metaphor signifies the greatness and mighty authority of Jesus, who is God the Word.

"And His face is shining like the sun in its power" (1:16, AT). In His resurrection, Jesus radiates the glory of the God of Psalm 84:11: "Yahweh God is a *sun* and shield…." Jesus is the fulfillment of the priestly blessing: "May Yahweh make His *face shine* upon you and be gracious to you" (Num. 6:25, AT). As Paul said, we see "the *light* of the knowledge of the glory of God in the *face* of Jesus Christ" (2 Cor. 4:6).

I AM the First and the Last. In that opening vision, Jesus said, "Do not be fearing; I AM the first and the last, and the living One,…" (1:17-18, AT, cf. 2:8, 22:13). Jesus used the same emphatic *egō eimi* that we studied in *The Gospel according to John*, alluding to Exodus 3:14-15. He followed His self-identification as Yahweh with another phrase used of Yahweh in Isaiah:

> Thus says Yahweh, the King of Israel
>   and his Redeemer, Yahweh of hosts:
> "I am the first, and I am the last;
>   besides me there is no god" (Isa. 44:6, cf. 41:4, 48:12).

Jesus is the Yahweh of Isaiah, the only God. "The first and the last" forms a merism, in which two poles signify the entire spectrum. It communicates that Yahweh, Jesus, is not only the originator of all things and their end-times consummator, but also the governor of every thing and event between the first and the last. He is sovereign over cosmic history.[66] G. K. Beale writes, "As in Isaiah, the expression functions in v 17b to assure John and his readers that Christ is in control of the vicissitudes of history,

---

"Toward a Systematic Theology of the Deity of Christ," in *The Deity of Christ*, 199-200.

64. Prov. 16:31, Lev. 19:32, cf. the judgment context of Dan. 7:9 (esp. v. 10).

65. Isa. 1:18, Rev. 7:14, 15:5, 19:8; *pace* Osborne, *Revelation*, 90, n. 9.

66. So also Osborne, *Revelation*, 95.

however bad they seem. Indeed, he is the force behind history, causing it to fulfill his purposes."[67]

"The living God" was a common designation for God,[68] and here Jesus is "the living One," (Rev. 1:18). Jesus, as the self-sufficient Yahweh the Son, has eternal life in Himself (cf. Jn. 1:4, 5:26). He continued, "I was dead, and behold, I am living into the ages of the ages…" (1:18, AT). In 4:9, 10, and 10:6, God the Father is "the One, living into the ages of the ages,"[69] so this opening revelation again stresses the unity of divine essence between the Father and Son as One eternal, sovereign God.

Alpha and Omega. God the Father identified Himself in Revelation 1:8, "I AM the Alpha and the Omega, says the Lord God, who is and was and is coming, the Almighty" (AT, cf. 21:6). *Alpha* and *omega* are the first and last letters of the Greek alphabet, a common merism in the ancient world to highlight everything in between. (Compare to our saying, "from A to Z.") Verse 7 had just prophesied the second coming of Christ. Then in verse 8 God the Father certified that revelation as the Almighty Lord who began history and is governing His story to His purposed conclusion in salvation through judgment.[70]

Not surprisingly, by this point, Jesus self-identified with the same title: "I am the Alpha and the Omega, the first and the last, the beginning and the end" (22:13). Beale states clearly the view of many commentators:

> Now all these titles, which are used in the OT of God, are combined and applied to Christ to highlight his deity. The titles

---

67. Beale, *Revelation*, 213.

68. Osborne (*Revelation*, 95) cites Josh. 3:10, Ps. 42:2, Hos. 1:10, Acts 14:15, Rom. 9:26.

69. Osborne, *Revelation*, 95. Beale (*Revelation*, 214) draws the connection to Deut. 32:40, Dan. 4:34 (Theod.), and 12:7.

70. So also Beale, *Revelation*, 199; Osborne, *Revelation*, 71, 73. After discussing *egō eimi*, "the Lord God," and "Almighty," Osborne concludes that "all of Rev. 1:8 looks to God as ruler over all of history, in control of this world and the next, with full authority over earthly and cosmic forces" (72).

figuratively connote the totality of polarity: Christ's presence at and sovereignty over the beginning of creation and over the end of creation are boldly stated in order to indicate that he is also present at and sovereign over all events in between. The emphasis of the bipolar names here at the end of the book is to underscore Christ's divine ability to conclude history at his coming.[71]

Jesus Christ is One with the Father. What the Father is, the Son is: Yahweh, the I AM, the Alpha and the Omega, King of kings and Lord of lords.

Worship. Given such a unified identification of the Father and Son, the book of Revelation fittingly shows Jesus as the recipient of the same worship as the Father, together as One worthy God. In chapter 4, the twenty-four elders surrounding God's throne constantly say, "Worthy are You, our Lord and God, to receive the glory and the honor and the power…" (4:11, AT). Chapter 5 then introduces "the Lion of the tribe of Judah, the Root of David" (v. 5). Jesus is not merely a Branch, a descendent of David; He is also the Root, the Creator of David.[72] Only the God-Man can be the Cause of His own ancestors! The Lion conquered because He is the Lamb having been slaughtered (Passover language), now standing alive again with the fullness of the Spirit of God (v. 6).

Then John saw the twenty-four elders fall down before the Lamb (the posture of worship, 5:9), singing a new song to the Lamb: "Worthy are You…" (v. 10), just as they sang to the Father in 4:11.

Then John beheld a vision of the end of the age:[73]

---

71. Beale, *Revelation*, 138. Cf. Osborne, *Revelation*, 789, employing similar language, concluding, "Since this is the only passage to contain all three titles, it has the greatest emphasis of them all on the all-embracing power of Christ over human history."

72. Isa. 11:1, 10

73. For a chart and explanation of the belief that each interlude in Revelation unveils information before or at the opening of the Great Tribulation, followed by information of the closing or aftermath, see page 7 of notes at ProjectOne28.com/rev5.

REVELATION 5:11-14 (AT)

[11]And I saw, and I heard the voice of many angels around the throne, and of the living creatures and of the elders, and their number was myriads of myriads and thousands of thousands, [12]saying in a great voice:

> "Worthy is the Lamb having been slaughtered to receive the power and wealth and wisdom and strength and honor and glory and blessing!"

[13]And I heard every creature which is in heaven and upon the earth and under the earth and upon the sea and all the things in them, saying:

> "To the One sitting upon the throne and to the Lamb be the blessing and the honor and the glory and the might into the ages of the ages!"

[14]And the four living creatures were saying, "Amen!" And the elders fell and worshiped.

In 5:12 the Lamb is worshiped by myriads of angels with the same language as the Father in 4:11: "Worthy... to receive... the power... honor and glory." Not only that, but 5:13 makes clear that every creature in the New Creation will worship the Father and the Son in the same breath!

This warrants Köstenberger's note: "The book of Revelation is supremely concerned with the difference between true and false worship."[74] False worship is strictly condemned as performed only by those whose names are not written in the Book of Life (13:8, 17:8). At the end of Revelation, an overwhelmed John fell down to worship the glorious angel before him, but the angel was jealous for the worship of God alone: "*Don't!* I am a fellow servant with you and your brothers, the ones holding to the witness of Jesus – worship God!" (19:10, AT[75]). No creature is worthy of worship. Only God deserves worship. And Jesus is worshiped. Jesus must not be a creature. Jesus must be God!

This is the "eternal Gospel" (14:6): "Revere God and give glory ˌto, Him, because the hour ˌof, His judgment has come, and worship the ˌOne who, made heaven and earth and sea and springs ˌof, waters" (14:7, AT). We must believe the good news that Jesus is God, who made heaven and earth and became flesh to die for sins and be raised again. We must honor the Son as we honor the Father in order to be the true worshipers sought by God.[76]

In the final vision of the new, heavenly earth, John saw the eternal reality: "And every cursed ˌthing, will be no longer. And the throne ˌof, God and the Lamb will be in it, and His servants will worship Him" (22:3, AT). Not two thrones. One throne, belonging to God and the Lamb (cf. 3:21). Not worship "Them." Worship "Him," singular. The New Testament does not advocate the worship of three gods. Richard Bauckham rightly states that Jesus "is worthy of divine worship because his worship can be included in the worship of the one God."[77] "Worship *Him,*" the Three-in-One God.

I AM the One Searching Hearts. In Revelation 2:23, Jesus warns of the result of His coming judgment on idolatrous "Christians": "all the assemblies will come to know that I AM the ˌOne, searching minds[78] and hearts, and I will give ˌto, each ˌof, you according to your works" (AT). Both clauses of searching and judging are common of Yahweh throughout the Old Testament, but they appear together

---

74. Köstenberger, "The Deity of Christ in John's Letters and the Book of Revelation," in *The Deity of Christ*, 162. Cf. Osborne, *Revelation*, 46-49.

75. The angel's first response, "ὅρα μή [*hora mē*] is best rendered literally as 'see not,' and is roughly equivalent with our colloquial 'Don't!'" (Beale, *Revelation*, 946, cf. 22:8-9).

76. Jn. 5:23 (cf. Lk. 10:16, Jn. 15:23; 1 Jn. 2:23; 2 Jn. 1:9), 4:23-24

77. *The Theology of the Book of Revelation* (Cambridge University Press, 1993), 60, qtd. in Köstenberger, "The Deity of Christ in John's Letters and the Book of Revelation," in *The Deity of Christ*, 163.

78. Lit., "kidneys," a common Hebraic metaphor (cf., e.g., ESV translation note in Jer. 17:10). "The remaining nine references all use kidneys as a symbol of the innermost being. This is probably so since in dismembering an animal the kidneys are the last organ to be reached. In this usage it is frequently paralleled with heart..." (John N. Oswalt, "*kilya*," *TWOT*, 441).

only in Jeremiah 17:10.[79] Jesus, again employing the emphatic I AM, assumed the ability of Yahweh alone: omniscient judgment. We may fool everyone else with hypocritical good works and hidden evil desires and deeds, but Jesus' eyes pierce to the depth of our inner being, and He will judge righteously the secrets He finds there (cf. Rom. 2:16).

Bringing My Recompense. In a similar warning, Jesus' concludes the book with, "Behold, I am coming quickly, and My recompense is, with Me, to repay to, each as his work is" (22:12, AT). Yahweh in flesh is the fulfillment of the promise in Isaiah 40:10 and 62:11 of *Adonai Yahweh* coming with recompense.[80] God the Son will execute the final judgment in concert with God the Father.[81] Are we ready? Have we washed our robes in the blood of the Lamb (22:14, 7:14)? Are we agreeing with His Spirit who works in us righteous deeds[82] that will be evidence on that Day of our new birth in Christ?

Receiving Prayer. "The Bible closes with a prayer to Jesus."[83] In Revelation 22:20 (AT), John wrote, "The One, bearing witness to these things, is saying, 'Yes, I am coming quickly.' *Amen, come Lord Jesus!*" This was not an anomaly. Praying to Jesus as God is common in Scripture. Jesus had invited us to pray for everything to Him, the God-Man, the only Mediator between God and Man (Jn. 14:13-14, cf. 1 Tim. 2:5). Christians, by definition, are those who call upon the Name of the *Lord* Jesus Christ in prayer for salvation (Acts 2:21, 9:14, 22:16; 1 Cor. 1:2; Rom. 10:13). Paul prayed to Christ three times to remove the thorn in his flesh and gladly

---

79. Beale, *Revelation*, 264.

80. Frame, *The Doctrine of God*, 653, where he also lists the allusion to the God of Ps. 62:12. Beale (*Revelation*, 1138) suggests a possible echo of Mt. 16:27.

81. Read Jn. 5:22, 27 (context: 5:18). Cf. both on the throne in Rev. 3:21, 20:11; Acts 17:31.

82. Rev. 19:8, cf. Gal. 2:20, 5:8, 22-23, Phil. 1:11, 2:12-13, Rom. 2:6-11, 7:4, 8:5, 13-14; Eph. 2:10.

83. Peterson, "Toward a Systematic Theology of the Deity of Christ," in *The Deity of Christ*, 205.

received His grace and power instead (2 Cor. 12:8-10). As Stephen was being stoned to death, "he called out, 'Lord Jesus, receive my spirit'" (Acts 7:59), like the psalmist did to Yahweh (31:5) and Jesus to the Father (Lk. 23:46). Robert Peterson comments: "Here, combined with a use of 'Lord' indicating divinity, is an urgent prayer directed to Jesus just as one would direct such a prayer to God. And that is the point. Praying to Jesus is praying to God."[84] John's closing prayer in Revelation also addressed Jesus as Lord, Yahweh become flesh. Let us believe as John believed and pray for the Day that we see Him as John saw Him.

"Amen, come Lord Jesus!"

---

84. *Ibid.*, 205.

Unto Worship & Witness

Brief review will serve the practical applications that follow.

In Chapter One, we learned the meaning inherent in the Name Yahweh through its correspondence with I AM who I AM. By choosing the Name Yahweh, God revealed Himself as eternal, unchanging, self-sufficient, sovereign, and free. In Chapter Two, we discussed the disobedience of the intertestamental Jews who piously replaced the Name Yahweh with *Adonai*, "Lord" (and later, *hashem*, "the Name"). That practice was followed in the Greek Old Testament (*kurios*), quoted by New Testament authors, and carried into our English Old Testaments with small-caps "Lord." Disciples were urged to obey Exodus 3:15, putting Yahweh into remembrance with reverence and delight.

In Chapter Three, we examined the fuller revelation of the Name, which He "made for Himself" in the Exodus: the One who fulfills His covenant promises by sovereignly dispensing judgment upon His enemies and mercifully redeeming His chosen people through substitutionary sacrifice.

In Chapter Four, we discovered Jesus' repeated "I AM" statements in the emphatic Greek translation of Exodus 3:14, claiming to be Yahweh. Because Jesus stated and demonstrated His eternal self-existence, we believe He was alive and active in the Old Testament as the image of the Triune God. Chapter Five showed that every Old Testament saint who saw God did not see the Father, but the Son. The Angel (Messenger) of Yahweh is Yahweh Himself, the Son sent by the Father in the fullness of His Godhood, to be worshiped and obeyed. We also highlighted some specific prophecies that the coming Messiah would be a God-Man, Yahweh in flesh.

In Chapter Six, we studied the Gospels to see that Yeshua's birth, ministry, death, and resurrection revealed His Godhood. At His virginal conception and birth, He was announced by angels as the Lord, Yahweh come to save. He followed the one who prepared the way for Yahweh. He said and did things that only God can do, such as forgiving sins and controlling creation. Even in flesh, disciples worshiped Him because His deity was in no way diminished. We savored the Scriptural contention that only the God-Man can reconcile God and Man. His crucifixion fulfilled the prophecy that Yahweh would be pierced for our transgressions, and His resurrection vindicated Him as the almighty Son of God, who deserves to be worshiped by all peoples.

Chapter Seven relayed the apostolic witness that Jesus is *theos* (God) and its application of Old Testament passages about the *kurios* (Yahweh) to Jesus. He is the Creator and Sustainer, the Alpha and the Omega, worshiped in the same manner as God the Father, soon bringing recompense as Yahweh of the prophets.

I have sought to be faithfully full in the presentation of Jesus' Godhood, but I do not pretend it is comprehensive. So many more Scriptures could be listed and explained because Jesus' Godhood is embedded into the fabric of the New Testament. Bowman and Komoszewski teach a clever acronym to remember the categories also contained in this book: Jesus shares the H.A.N.D.S. of God.[1] That is, Jesus shares in the *H*onors, *A*ttributes, *N*ames, *D*eeds, and *S*eat that belongs to God and God alone – because He is One with the Father and Spirit.

So what?

Everything. Nothing could be more relevant than the Godhood of Jesus. Every cubic millimeter of the universe is claimed by the Lord Jesus Christ. Every millisecond of your life is purposed for His glory. Every thought and deed will be weighed by Him. Every ounce of eternal joy is offered only through Him.

Jesus is Yahweh the Son, and besides Him, there is no Savior. Do you believe He was pierced for our transgressions, buried, and raised on the third day? Do you honor God the Son as you honor God the Father? Do you hold the light of the knowledge of the glory of God in the face of Jesus Christ (2 Cor. 4:6) as an infinitely valuable treasure (4:7)? Do you consider all else to be dung compared to the surpassing value of knowing Christ Jesus as your Lord (Phil. 3:8)? Or do you mix hot and cold water and live lukewarm?

We must not let our "Jesus Is My Homeboy" culture cloud the overwhelming reality that our friendship with Jesus remains one of a finite, humble disciple to an infinite, sovereign Lord. Jesus said, "You are my friends if you do what I command you" (Jn. 15:14).[2] We must not be among the fools who call Him, "Lord, Lord," but do not do what He says (Lk. 6:46). If we hear His words and

---

1. *Putting Jesus in His Place: The Case for the Deity of Christ*, a resource to which I was pointed by Peterson, "Toward a Systematic Theology of the Deity of Christ," in *The Deity of Christ*, 194.

2. D. A. Carson: "Certainly such friendship is not reciprocal. I cannot turn around to Jesus and thank him for his friendship and tell him he is my friend, too, if he does everything I command him. Strange to tell, not once is Jesus or God ever described in the Bible as our friend. Abraham is God's friend; the reverse is never stated" (*The Difficult Doctrine of the Love of God* [Wheaton, IL: Crossway, 2000], 41; see pp. 41-43 for Carson's helpful commentary on our friendship to Jesus).

do not put them into practice, our destruction will be complete (6:47-49). But if we obey, His joy will be in us, and so our joy will be complete (Jn. 15:11).

The God-breathed truths reported in this study should stir us to worship the Three-in-One God. How could we not? The incarnation of God the Son is the most astounding mystery of the faith. Fresh revelation of God's glory in Christ overflows into joyous praise. Spontaneous, Spirit-birthed praise then leads to a Spiritual lifestyle of worship: "Therefore, I am encouraging you, brothers, by the mercies of God, to offer your bodies as a sacrifice, living, holy, and, pleasing to God, your logical worship" (Rom. 12:1, AT). Since Jesus is God the Son, it only makes sense to serve Him with unqualified allegiance and wholehearted obedience. Let us all be growing as Jesus' disciples who keep as much as everything He commanded and who make disciples by teaching them to keep as much as everything He commanded (Mt. 28:18-20).[3]

These God-breathed truths will affect our evangelism as the truths in *Part One* also do.[4] There we saw that it would be inappropriate to deliver the gospel as an appeal to self-preservation: "Use Jesus to get out of hell and into heaven." The Biblical context of "the gospel of the glory of Jesus Christ" (2 Cor. 4:4-6) is the glory of God in Jesus Christ. He is the greatest value, and He does all things for the greatest reason: the glory of His Name. He came to save us for His Name's sake, that all nations may glorify God for His mercy.[5] After the facts of the good news – that God sent His Son who died for sins and was raised again – the proper appeal is, in essence: "Repent of your selfishness, submit to Christ's Lordship, trust in His gracious sacrifice, and experience fullness of joy *by glorifying Him* now and forever."

---

3. See *Introduction to Disciple-making* (free at ProjectOne28.com/i2dm).

4. For this paragraph, see esp. Chapter Four, "Saved for Glory," and Chapter Five, "Disciples for Glory," in *Part One,* esp. 61-66 (free at ProjectOne28.com/glory).

5. E.g., Isa. 43:25, 60:21, 61:3; Rom. 1:5, 15:7-9; 1 Jn. 2:12; Ps. 25:11, 109:21, 79:9, Jer. 14:7, 21.

The clarity of *Part Two* should cause us to avoid a lowest common denominator kind of evangelism. Sometimes the church can fall into thinking, "What is the least a person needs to understand to truly believe the gospel and be saved?" Why not aim for a fuller presentation? At least, we must include the Godhood of the Man Christ Jesus. Some presentations remain content to portray Jesus as Man without clarifying that He is the God-Man. But here we read Jesus' own words, literally, "Unless you believe that *I AM*, you will die in your sins" (Jn. 8:24). We read Paul, contextually, "If you confess with your mouth Jesus to be, *Lord* and believe in your heart that God raised Him from the dead, you will be saved…. Because 'everyone who calls upon the Name of the Lord [*Yahweh*, quoting Joel 2:32] will be saved'" (Rom. 10:9, 13, AT). In order to be saved, we must believe that Jesus is Yahweh the Son, not merely a human agent through whom God saves.

I am not suggesting that every convert must hear and understand the Hebrew Name *Yahweh* (though that would be best). Neither am I suggesting that every convert must be able to explain Chalcedonian Trinitarianism (though he should soon be equipped for it[6]). But if the evangelized person is asked, "Do you believe that the Man Christ Jesus is God the Son?" and he responds, "No, I think he is just a man," then that person will not be saved, unless he repents and embraces the truth.[7] We must soberly remember how the Scriptures regularly characterized unbelief in terms of being blinded to Jesus' Godhood because of fixation on His Manhood: "Isn't this the carpenter's son?"[8]

John Stott is right: "Nobody can call himself a Christian who does not worship Jesus. To worship him, if he is not God, is idolatry; to withhold worship from him, if he is, is apostasy."[9]

---

6. See ProjectOne28.com/chalcedon.

7. For the possibility of fuzzy understanding, but the impossibility of such a denial, see John Piper, "What Must I Do To Be Saved?" (Episode 325), Ask Pastor John, 22 Apr 2014 (soundcloud.com/askpastorjohn/what-must-i-believe-to-be-saved-episode-325).

8. E.g., Mt. 13:53-58, Mk. 6:1-6, Lk. 4:22, Jn. 6:41-42.

Therefore, we must prepare ourselves to faithfully, lovingly, and persuasively present Jesus as the eternal I AM who became the God-Man to die, rise, call, justify, and glorify sinners in Himself.[10] We must bid them bow and bellow, "Jesus Christ is Yahweh!" – to the glory of God the Father (Phil. 2:10-11). And we must watch our own life and doctrine closely, that we, too, may gain the prize.[11]

It is my earnest prayer that this brief study will thus impact our lives for obedient worship and faithful witness. *Spirit of Christ, please make it so!*

---

9.   John R. W. Stott, *The Authentic Jesus* (London: Marshall, Morgan & Scott, 1985), 34, qtd. in Wellum, "The Deity of Christ in the Apostolic Witness," in *The Deity of Christ*, 142, as well as Bowman and Komoszewski, *Putting Jesus in His Place*, 42.

10. 1 Pet. 3:15; recall the Scriptural logic of the early church fathers, like Athanasius, explained and cited on pages 112-113.

11. 1 Tim. 4:16; 1 Cor. 9:27

ACKNOWLEDGMENTS

I first taught publicly about the Name Yahweh, its mistranslation, and Jesus' self-identification as the I AM in a small Sunday night setting on March 28, 2010. I can still remember it, and I listened to the recording recently. From a human standpoint, the presentation was weak. But the truth was power. That night the Spirit confirmed in me the sense I had that He was assigning me to proclaim the Name above all names. I am grateful to have been surrounded then by saints like Sam McVay, Jr., Quincey and Willa Barnard, and Levi Keplar, who were able to give me the kind of spiritual encouragement about the teaching that guarded me from pride and focused me on the Spirit's jealousy to glorify Jesus as Yahweh. May that ever be the case!

More recently, with regard to this book, I am grateful to my dear brothers Mick Murray and Dr. Brock McKay for their early review and encouragements. Not only the skill in the cover design and website development, but even more the faithful friendship of Tyler Norris continually enriches my labors and my life. I am especially grateful to Heather Trent Beers for her graciousness and helpfulness in editing and improving this work. Any enduring errors or weaknesses, of course, belong not to her, but to me.

My wife Amber is my favorite. She is the best I have of this earthly life. Her merciful and faithful ministry at home and her support for me in and out of the home give me such stability, strength, and joy.

To the Father of every good gift be all glory now and into the ages!

SELECT BIBLIOGRAPHY

Athanasius, *De Synodis* 51 (ccel.org/ccel/schaff/npnf204.xxii.ii.iii.html).

Bauer, William, *A Greek-English Lexicon of the New Testament and Other Early Christian Literature,* Third Edition, Rev. and ed. Frederick William Danker (Chicago and London: The University of Chicago Press, 2000).

Beale, G. K., "An Exegetical and Theological Consideration of the Hardening of Pharaoh's Heart in Exodus 4-14 and Romans 9," *Trinity Journal* 5 NS (1984), 129-154.

—— *The Book of Revelation,* The New International Greek Testament Commentary (Grand Rapids, MI: Eerdmans, 1999).

Bietenhard, Hans, "Angel, Messenger," *New International Dictionary of New Testament Theology*, ed. Colin Brown (Grand Rapids, MI: Zondervan, 1986), 1:101-103.

—— "Lord, Master," *New International Dictionary of New Testament Theology*, ed. Colin Brown (Grand Rapids, MI: Zondervan, 1986), 2:512.

Bird, Michael, "Of God, Angels, and Men," *How God Became Jesus: The Real Origins of Belief in Jesus' Divine Nature – A Response to Bart Ehrman*, ed. Michael F. Bird (Grand Rapids, MI: Zondervan, 2014).

Bowling, Andrew, "*mal'āk*," *Theological Wordbook of the Old Testament,* ed. R. Laird Harris, Gleason L. Archer, Jr., and Bruce K. Waltke (Chicago, IL: Moody Publishers, 1980), 465.

Bowman, Jr., Robert M., and J. Ed Komoszewski, *Putting Jesus in His Place: The Case for the Deity of Christ* (Grand Rapids, MI: Kregel, 2007).

Brown, Colin, "God, Gods, Emmanuel," *New International Dictionary of New Testament Theology*, ed. Colin Brown (Grand Rapids, MI: Zondervan, 1986), 2:69.

Brown, Francis, S. R. Driver, and Charles A. Briggs. *The New Brown-Driver-Briggs-Gesenius Hebrew and English Lexicon* (Peabody, Mass.: Hendrickson, 1979).

Carson, D. A., *Matthew*, The Expositor's Bible Commentary, Vol. 8, ed.

Frank E. Gæbelein (Grand Rapids, MI: Zondervan, 1984).

—— *The Difficult Doctrine of the Love of God* (Wheaton, IL: Crossway, 2000).

—— *The Gospel according to John,* The Pillar New Testament Commentary, ed. D. A. Carson (Grand Rapids, MI: Eerdmans, 1991).

Chafer, Lewis Sperry, *Systematic Theology*, Vol. 3-4 (Grand Rapids: Kregel, 1976).

Childs, Brevard, *The Book of Exodus: A Critical, Theological Commentary* (Philadelphia: Westminster, 1974).

Clendenen, E. Ray, "When and Why Do We Update Bible Translations?" (biblegateway.com/perspectives-in-translation/2010/12/when-and-why-do-we-update-bible-translations-e-ray-clendenen/).

Cohen, Abraham, *Everyman's Talmud* (New York: E. P. Dutton & Co., 1932).

Comfort, Philip W., & Wendell C. Hawley, *1-3 John,* Cornerstone Biblical Commentary, ed. Philip W. Comfort (Carol Stream, IL: Tyndale House, 2007).

Currid, John, *Ancient Egypt and the Old Testament* (Grand Rapids, MI: Baker Books, 1997).

—— *Exodus*, Vol. 1: Chapters 1-18, Evangelical Press Study Commentary (Auburn, MA: Evangelical Press, 2000).

—— *Genesis*, Vol. 1: Genesis 1:1–25:18, Evangelical Press Study Commentary (Darlington, England: Evangelical Press, 2003).

Dennis, Lane T. et al., ed., *ESV Study Bible, English Standard Version* (Wheaton, IL: Crossway, 2008).

Driver, S. R., *The Book of Exodus* (Cambridge: University Press, 1929).

Durham, John, *Exodus*, Word Biblical Commentary (Nashville: Thomas Nelson, 1987).

Frame, John M., *The Doctrine of God* (Phillipsburg, NJ: P&R Publishing, 2002).

Gathercole, Simon, *The Preexistent Son: Recovering the Christologies of Matthew, Mark, and Luke* (Grand Rapids, MI: Eerdmans, 2006).

Geisler, Norman L., *Baker Encyclopedia of Christian Apologetics* (Grand Rapids, MI: Baker Books, 1999).

Grudem, Wayne, *Systematic Theology: An Introduction to Biblical Doctrine* (Grand Rapids, MI: Zondervan, 1994).

Hamilton, Jr., James M., *With the Clouds of Heaven: The Book of Daniel in Biblical Theology*, New Studies in Biblical Theology, ed. D. A. Carson (Downers Grove, IL: InterVarsity Press, 2014).

Hamilton, Victor P., *"shadday," Theological Wordbook of the Old Testament,* ed. R. Laird Harris, Gleason L. Archer, Jr., and Bruce K. Waltke (Chicago, IL: Moody Publishers, 1980), 907.

Harris, Murray J., *Prepositions and Theology in the Greek New Testament: An Essential Reference Resource for Exegesis* (Grand Rapids, MI: Zondervan, 2012).

Holman Christian Standard Bible® Copyright © 2003, 2002, 2000, 1999 by Holman Bible Publishers. Used by permission. All rights reserved.

Holy Bible, New International Version®. Copyright © 1973, 1978, 1984 Biblica. Used by permission of Zondervan. All rights reserved.

Holy Bible, New Living Translation, copyright © 1996, 2004, 2007 by Tyndale House Foundation. Used by permission of Tyndale House Publishers, Inc., Carol Stream, Illinois 60188. All rights reserved.

Isbell, Charles D., *"peˡlah," Theological Wordbook of the Old Testament,* ed. R. Laird Harris, Gleason L. Archer, Jr., and Bruce K. Waltke (Chicago, IL: Moody Publishers, 1980), 1059.

Juncker, Günther, "Christ As Angel: The Reclamation of a Primitive Title," *Trinity Journal* 15:2 (Fall 1994): 221-250.

Köstenberger, Andreas, "The Deity of Christ in John's Gospel," *The Deity of Christ,* ed. Christopher W. Morgan & Robert A. Peterson (Wheaton, IL: Crossway, 2011).

—— "The Deity of Christ in John's Letters and the Book of Revelation," *The Deity of Christ,* ed. Christopher W. Morgan & Robert A. Peterson (Wheaton, IL: Crossway, 2011).

Ladd, George Eldon, *A Theology of the New Testament,* Revised Edition, ed. Donald A. Hagner (Grand Rapids: Eerdmans, 1993).

Lister, Rob, *God Is Impassible and Impassioned: Toward a Theology of Divine Emotion* (Wheaton, IL: Crossway, 2013).

Literal Translation of the Holy Bible, Copyright © 1976-2000 Jay P. Green. Used by permission.

McDonough, Sean M., *YHWH at Patmos: Rev. 1:4 in Its Hellenistic and Early Jewish Setting* (Tübingen: Mohr Siebeck, 1999).

McGrath, Alister E., *Historical Theology: An Introduction to the History of Christian Thought,* Second Ed. (West Sussex, UK: Wiley-Blackwell, 2013).

McVay, Jr., Sam, and Spencer Stewart, *Introduction to Disciple-making: Obeying the Global Mandate of the Resurrected King Jesus* (El Dorado, KS: Project one28, 2013).

—— *The Kingdom of God: The Reason Christ Created Man, Became Man, and Is Coming Again* (El Dorado, KS: Project one28, 2010).

—— *The Model Prayer: Jesus Said, "Be Praying in This Manner"* (El Dorado, KS: Project one28, 2013).

Metzger, Bruce, *A Textual Commentary on the Greek New Testament,* Second Ed. (Stuttgart: German Bible Society, 1994).

Moo, Douglas J., *The Epistle to the Romans,* New International Commentary on the New Testament (Grand Rapids, MI: Eerdmans, 1996).

Moore, Rev. George F. "Jehovah," *The Encyclopaedia Britannica,* Vol. XV, 11th Ed. (Cambridge: University Press, 1911).

Motyer, J. Alec, *The Message of Exodus,* The Bible Speaks Today (Downers Grove, IL: InterVarsity Press, 2005).

—— *The Prophecy of Isaiah: An Introduction & Commentary* (Downers Grove, IL: IVP Academic, 1993).

—— "The Revelation of the Divine Name" (Tyndale Press, 1959), now free at TheologicalStudies.org.uk/article_revelation_motyer.html.

Nichols, Stephen J., "The Deity of Christ Today," *The Deity of Christ*, ed. Christopher W. Morgan & Robert A. Peterson (Wheaton, IL: Crossway, 2011).

Norton, Mark R., "Texts and Manuscripts of the Old Testament," *The Origin of the Bible*, ed. Philip Comfort (Carol Stream, IL: Tyndale House, 2003).

O'Brien, Peter T., *The Letter to the Ephesians,* The Pillar New Testament Commentary (Grand Rapids, MI: Eerdmans, 1999).

—— *The Letter to the Hebrews,* The Pillar New Testament Commentary (Grand Rapids, MI: Eerdmans, 2010).

Ortlund, Jr., Raymond, "The Deity of Christ and the Old Testament," *The Deity of Christ,* ed. Christopher W. Morgan & Robert A. Peterson (Wheaton, IL: Crossway, 2011).

Osborne, Grant R., *Matthew*, Zondervan Exegetical Commentary on the New Testament, ed. Clinton E. Arnold (Grand Rapids, MI: Zondervan, 2010).

—— *Revelation,* Baker Exegetical Commentary on the New Testament (Grand Rapids, MI: Baker Academic, 2002)

—— *The Gospel of John,* Cornerstone Biblical Commentary, ed. Philip W. Comfort (Carol Stream, IL: Tyndale House, 2007).

Oswalt, John N., "*kilya*," *Theological Wordbook of the Old Testament,* ed. R. Laird Harris, Gleason L. Archer, Jr., and Bruce K. Waltke (Chicago, IL: Moody Publishers, 1980), 441.

Parke-Taylor, G. H., *Yahweh: The Divine Name in the Bible* (Waterloo, Ontario: Wilfrid Laurier University Press, 1975).

Payne, J. Barton, "*yhwh*," *Theological Wordbook of the Old Testament,* ed. R. Laird Harris, Gleason L. Archer, Jr., and Bruce K. Waltke (Chicago, IL:

Moody Publishers, 1980), 210-212.

Peterson, Robert A., "Toward a Systematic Theology of the Deity of Christ," *The Deity of Christ*, ed. Christopher W. Morgan & Robert A. Peterson (Wheaton, IL: Crossway, 2011).

Piper, John, *Desiring God: Meditations of a Christian Hedonist* (Sisters, OR: Multnomah, 2003).

—— *Future Grace: The Purifying Power of the Promises of God*, Revised Ed. (Colorado Springs: Multnomah Books, 2012).

—— "He Knew What Was In Man," 11 Jan 2009 (desiringGod.org/sermons/he-knew-what-was-in-man).

—— "I Am the Light of the World," 12 Mar 2011 (desiringGod.org/sermons/i-am-the-light-of-the-world).

—— "I Am Who I Am," 16 Sept 1984 (desiringGod.org/sermons/i-am-who-i-am).

—— "In The Beginning Was the Word," 21 Sept 2008 (desiringgod.org/sermons/in-the-beginning-was-the-word).

—— "Prolegomena To Understanding Romans 9:14-15: An Interpretation of Exodus 33:19," *The Journal of the Evangelical Theological Society* 22/3 (1979).

—— "The Truth Will Set You Free," 19 Mar 2011 (desiringGod.org/sermons/the-truth-will-set-you-free).

—— "What Must I Do To Be Saved?" (Episode 325), Ask Pastor John, 22 Apr 2014 (soundcloud.com/askpastorjohn/what-must-i-believe-to-be-saved-episode-325).

Rengstorf, K. H., "Jesus Christ, Nazarene, Christian," *New International Dictionary of New Testament Theology*, ed. Colin Brown (Grand Rapids, MI: Zondervan, 1986), 2:330-332.

Robinson, D. W. B., "Church," *New Bible Dictionary*, Third Ed., ed. D. R. W. Wood (Downers Grove, IL: Inter-Varsity Press, 1996), 199-202.

Rogers, Anthony, "Let Us Make Man: A Trinitarian Interpretation" (answeringislam.org/authors/rogers/genesis_1_26_trinitarian.html).

Sarna, Nahum, *Genesis*, The JPS Torah Commentary (Philadelphia: The Jewish Publication Society, 1989).

Scott, Jack B., *"elōhîm,"* *Theological Wordbook of the Old Testament*, ed. R. Laird Harris, Gleason L. Archer, Jr., and Bruce K. Waltke (Chicago, IL: Moody Publishers, 1980), 41-44.

Steinmann, Andrew E., Daniel (St. Louis, MO: Concordia Publishing House, 2008).

Stewart, Spencer, "A Celebration of Propitiation," 29 Mar 2013 (ProjectOne28.com/propitiation).

—— "Daniel 10: God-given Revelation of the Heavenly/Earthly War," 2 Sept 2012 (ProjectOne28.com/Dan10).

—— "Introduction to the Old Testament" (ProjectOne28.com/ OTsurvey).

—— *Light Shines in the Darkness: Scripture Interpreting the Spiritual Drama of Genesis 1:2-3* (El Dorado, KS: Project one28, 2010).

—— "Plagues on All the Egyptian gods" (ProjectOne28.com/plagues).

—— "The Doctrine of God" (ProjectOne28.com/doctrine-of-God).

—— *The Preeminence of Christ: Part One, To the Glory of God the Father,* Second Edition (Lawrence, KS: Project one28, 2017).

—— "The Son of Man and the Saints of the Most High," 2 Feb 2012 (ProjectOne28.com/Son_of_Man).

—— *Theology 101 for Kids!* (ProjectOne28.com/kids).

—— "Tying the Two Testaments Together" (ProjectOne28.com/two-testaments).

Stott, John R. W., *The Cross of Christ*, 20th Anniversary Edition (Downers Grove, IL: IVP Books, 2006).

The Jewish Encyclopedia, ed. Isidore Singer (New York: Ktav Publishing House, 1906).

The NET Bible, Copyright © 1996-2005 Biblical Studies Press. Used by permission.

The New American Standard Bible®, Copyright © 1960, 1962, 1963, 1968, 1971, 1972, 1973, 1975, 1977, 1995 by The Lockman Foundation. Used by permission.

The New King James Version. Copyright © 1982 by Thomas Nelson, Inc. Used by permission. All rights reserved.

Tigay, Jeffrey, *Deuteronomy*, JPS Torah Commentary (Philadelphia: Jewish Publication Society, 1996).

Wallace, Daniel B., *Greek Grammar Beyond the Basics: An Exegetical Syntax of the New Testament* (Grand Rapids, MI: Zondervan, 1996).

Wallace, Ronald, *The Message of Daniel,* The Bible Speaks Today (Downers Grove: IVP, 1984).

Walvoord, John, "Series in Christology – Part 4: The Preincarnate Son of God" (walvoord.com/article/31).

Wax, Trevin, "The Meaning of 'Maranatha,'" 2 Feb 2012 (thegospelcoalition. org/blogs/trevinwax/2012/02/02/the-meaning-of-maranatha/).

Weima, Jeffrey A. D., "1-2 Thessalonians," *Commentary on the New Testament Use of the Old Testament*, ed. G. K. Beale and D. A. Carson (Grand Rapids, MI: Baker Academic, 2007), 871-889.

Wells, David, *The Person of Christ: A Biblical and Historical Analysis of the Incarnation* (Wheaton, IL: Crossway, 1984).

Wellum, Stephen J., "The Deity of Christ in the Synoptic Gospels," *The Deity of Christ*, ed. Christopher W. Morgan & Robert A. Peterson (Wheaton, IL: Crossway, 2011).

Wuest, Kenneth S., *The New Testament: An Expanded Translation* (Grand Rapids, MI: Eerdmans, 1961, 1994).

SELECT SCRIPTURE INDEX

The Preeminence of Christ:
Part One, To the Glory of God the Father

Introduction to Disciple-making:
Obeying the Global Mandate of the Resurrected King Jesus

The Basics:
The Beginning, the Gospel of God's Grace, and the New Beginning

The Kingdom of God:
The Reason Christ Created Man, Became Man, and Is Coming Again

Light Shines in the Darkness:
Scripture Interpreting the Spiritual Drama of Genesis 1:2-3

Spirit, Soul, Body:
The Blueprint of Man in the Image of God

Spiritual Gifts:
Discovering Graces and Partnering to Manifest the Fullness of Christ

The Model Prayer:
Jesus Said, "Be Praying In This Manner"

Why Trust the Bible?

Theology 101 for Kids!

Free at ProjectOne28.com